AF488189

THE
MIRROR

The Mirror

© 2026 Shiv Somashekhar

All rights reserved.

No part of this publication may be reproduced, distributed, or transmitted in any form or by any means, including photocopying, recording, or other electronic or mechanical methods, without the prior written permission of the publisher, except in the case of brief quotations embodied in reviews and certain other noncommercial uses permitted by copyright law.

For permissions requests, contact inquiry@maros.art.

ISBN: 979-8-9949640-0-2 (hardcover)

First published 2026

Maros
Allen, Texas

Publisher's Cataloging-in-Publication Data

Names: Somashekhar, Shiv, author.
Title: The mirror: clarity over comfort / Shiv Somashekhar.
Description: Includes index. | First edition. | Allen, TX: Maros, 2026.
Identifiers: ISBN: 979-8-9949640-0-2 (hardcover) 979-8-9949640-1-9 (paperback) 979-8-9949640-2-6 (ebook)
Subjects: LCSH Self-actualization (Psychology). | Self-realization. | Conduct of life. | Self help. | BISAC SELF-HELP / Personal Growth / General
Classification: LCC BF637.S4 S66 2026 | DDC 158.1--dc23

THE MIRROR

CLARITY OVER COMFORT

SHIV SOMASHEKHAR

To Ganesh Somashekhar

Table of Contents

PART I:

THE FRAMEWORK

I.

Introduction

There are more things, Lucilius, likely to frighten us than there are to crush us; we suffer more often in imagination than in reality. —Seneca, Letters to Lucilius

These words are not true because Seneca wrote them. He wrote them because they were true. Two thousand years have not changed that. We still fail to see what is actually good. We still confuse what we can change with what we cannot, and exhaust ourselves fighting in the wrong places.

Life contains both good and bad — as true for someone comfortable as for someone in genuine difficulty. The good is real: health that holds, people who show up, work that sustains, a sense of self that feels solid. The bad is real: pain that persists, relationships that strain, financial weight that refuses to lift, questions about who you are that will not resolve. Most people carry some measure of both yet see neither clearly. The good goes unappreciated because it is quiet. The bad goes misunderstood — its causes misidentified, the line between what can be changed and what cannot never drawn.

This book — the mirror — is about clarity. About seeing what is actually there. What clarity produces, when the mirror is held honestly, is two things: the recognition of what is genuinely good — the people, the health, the steadiness that go unnoticed because they have never been absent — and the ending of pain that was never necessary. Not all pain is avoidable. But much of what exhausts people is: the inherited anxiety that has no real object, the fight against a fact that will not change, the standard assembled from elsewhere and never questioned. Seeing clearly does not make the unavoidable less real. It makes the avoidable visible — so that the energy spent on it can go somewhere that actually needs it.

The mirror works through three components. The first is four paths — appreciation, discontinuation, agency, and acceptance — which together describe every relationship a person can have with any feature of their experience. The second is three question sets, each shaped to a distinct part of your life in time, that identify which path applies. The third is five dimensions — physical well-being, emotional well-being, financial well-being, connections, and identity — which map the full territory of a human life. Each dimension contains facets: specific, narrow parts of your life where the questions produce clear answers. Clarity is about seeing the right paths.

Part I lays the foundation — the four paths, the questions, the dimensions, and how to find the right facet when the picture is unclear. Read it first. Part II examines each dimension in turn, covering past, present, and future within each — and its chapters can be entered in any order, starting with whatever dimension feels most pressing. Part III addresses the harder cases: problems that span dimensions, paths that conflict, and answers that have changed since you last looked. The Appendix addresses the framework's underlying structure for readers who want to understand why it is built the way it is.

This is not a book about motivation. It makes no promises about transformation. The cases that fill these pages are not decoration - they are the point. An abstract principle understood in the mind is not the same as a principle recognized in a life. The cases are how the framework becomes real.

The dimension chapters apply the same framework consistently and by design. The repetition is deliberate. A pattern understood once and possibly forgotten eventually is not the same as a pattern that stays with you — and the goal is that after enough cases and enough consistency, the questions become reflexive rather than effortful.

II.

The Four Paths

The four paths describe every relationship a person can have with any feature of their experience. Each one follows from seeing that feature clearly. The choosing remains yours.

Appreciation

When something is going well, the path is appreciation. This means seeing that a part of your life is working, naming it, and recognizing its value.

Negativity bias works against this. Your survival instinct has wired you to find what is wrong before what is right. A body that carries you through your days without complaint, a relationship that holds without drama, financial stability that covers your needs — these things become invisible through familiarity, the way you stop hearing a clock in a room you have been sitting in for hours. The first question corrects for this. Before examining what is wrong, it asks what is working.

When you are always climbing toward the next thing, the ground you stand on disappears from view. Appreciation is the habit of letting what you already have remain visible.

Appreciation is active. It includes the ongoing maintenance of what works — the investment in a relationship that is healthy, the habits that sustain your physical well-being, the financial discipline that keeps your security intact. What you tend, you keep.

Discontinuation

When something is not going well but does not truly matter, the path is discontinuation. This means recognizing that you have been spending energy — emotional, mental, practical — on something unworthy of it, and choosing to stop.

Much of what occupies attention does not deserve it. The anxiety that has no real object. The standard absorbed from somewhere else and never questioned. The pursuit of a goal that, when examined, you never actually wanted. The energy consumed by these concerns is real even when the concerns themselves are not. Discontinuation exists to recover it.

Recognizing that something lacks real weight and actually releasing it are different acts. You may know that a particular criticism misrepresents you and still feel it land. You may know that a particular comparison carries no genuine consequence and still make it. The recognition is intellectual. The release is emotional. The gap between them can be wide, and noticing the gap without judgment is part of the work.

When you arrive at discontinuation and find you cannot let go, this is information rather than failure. Sometimes the grip loosens once you stop feeding it attention. Sometimes it asks for time. When it persists despite sustained effort, it often has roots elsewhere — an emotional pattern, an identity question, an old wound — and the path may shift from discontinuation to acceptance.

Agency

When something is not going well, truly matters, and is within your control to change, the path is agency.

Agency takes different forms depending on the situation. Sometimes it means direct action: a conversation you have been avoiding, a habit you need to change, a decision you need to make. Sometimes it means structural change — reorganizing the conditions that produced the problem rather than address-ing the problem itself. And sometimes the path forward is staged: you see what needs to change but cannot change it all at once, and so you build toward it, saving before you can leave a job, recovering before you can address a relationship, laying groundwork before you can make a move.

The conclusion that nothing can be changed often arrives too early — change may be difficult, or past effort may have failed, but difficulty and failure are not the same as impossibility. The third question asks what is actually possible given your circumstances — not what is easy, not what has worked before, but what remains genuinely available.

Acceptance

When something is not going well, truly matters, and is not within your control to change, the path is acceptance.

Acceptance is a redirection of will — a reorientation, distinct from resignation. Resignation collapses at the fact. Acceptance redirects beyond it — asking what can be done with what remains. A person who accepts a chronic illness has released the expectation that today's limitations will be erased tomorrow — and recovered their energy for everything else.

Acceptance has a specific scope. A person permanently injured in an accident who then advocates for better safety standards is not fighting the unchangeable — the injury requires acceptance, but the advocacy is agency directed at something that can be changed. It does not release the grief.

Acceptance is a present-tense reading, open to revision as circumstances change. What is beyond your control today may be within your control tomorrow.

The Complete Set

These four paths are exhaustive. Appreciation operates on what is good. Discontinuation redirects attention from what does not deserve it. Agency operates on what is bad, matters, and is changeable. Acceptance operates on what is bad, matters, and is not changeable. Each occupies a different logical position, and together they cover every relationship a person can have with any feature of their experience. There is no fifth path.

The four paths describe your relationship to your experience. What you are appreciating, discontinuing, acting on, or accepting was shaped by conditions that preceded your choices — the family you were born into, the circumstances you inherited, the advantages and constraints that were in place before you were old enough to decide anything. Appreciation without that recognition tips toward self-congratulation. Agency without it tips toward self-blame when effort falls short. Acceptance without it can mistake a structural constraint for a personal failure. The examination is yours. The conditions were never entirely yours alone.

They hold across time as well. The same four paths apply to the present, the past, and the future. What changes is not the paths but the questions that identify which one applies. The next chapter is that work.

III.

The Three Questions

The four paths follow from seeing clearly. The question sets are how you get there. Asked in sequence, they narrow the field until a single path remains. The order holds because each question depends on the answer to the one before it.

The Present

What is the case, and what should I do about it?

The first question: Is it going well?

When you examine a facet of your life, the instinct is to look for what is wrong — to scan for problems and gaps. The first question asks whether the thing you are looking at is working. Whether it is functioning well enough that it supports your life rather than straining it.

When the answer is yes, the path is appreciation.

Every facet of life fluctuates — energy dips during a stressful week, a relationship strains during a difficult period, finances tighten after an unexpected expense. The first question asks about the general condition, not the current weather. A temporary low in a facet that is fundamentally sound is different from a sustained decline, and treating one as the other sends the examination in the wrong direction.

The second question: Does it truly matter?

You arrive here only when something is not going well. The second question asks whether what is not going well actually affects your life in a meaningful way — whether it carries real weight.

Some of what burdens you is genuinely consequential. Some is inherited anxiety, social comparison, or a habit of worry that attached itself to an unworthy target — and when the answer is no, the path is discontinuation.

Two tests sharpen the answer. If this problem disappeared, would your daily life actually change? Is this concern yours, or did you absorb it — a family standard, a cultural ideal, someone else's measure of a good life?

Sometimes a concern that does not truly matter has produced consequences that do. A long-running anxiety about status may not deserve your energy — the object does not matter — but if that anxiety has disrupted your sleep, strained your relationships, or produced chronic stress, those consequences are real and do matter. In such cases, discontinue the concern and turn the first question on its effects: is my sleep going well? Are my relationships going well? The concern and its effects may require different paths.

The third question: Is it in my control to change?

You arrive here only when something is not going well and it truly matters. The third question asks whether you have the ability to change it — whether you, given your actual circumstances and resources, can act on it.

A necessary candor: the question "is it in my control?" is shaped by circumstances that are not evenly distributed. Poverty, discrimination, disability, illness, caregiving obligations, and systemic inequality all constrain agency in ways that have nothing to do with effort or character. A person who cannot leave a bad job because they have no savings is not less capable than someone who can. They are less free. When the answer to the third question is no, the reason matters — and the questions lead away from self-blame toward an honest accounting of what is available.

Often the answer is partial. You can influence some aspects of a situation but not others. You can change your own behavior but not someone else's. Partial control, examined closely, resolves into a mosaic of specific answers. Break the situation into its parts and ask the third question about each one. "Is my chronic pain in my control?" is too broad. "Is my medication adherence in my control?" — yes, and that is agency. "Is the disease progression in my control?" — no, and that is acceptance.

The Past

What happened, and how should I carry it?

The same questions apply to the past, asked in the same sequence. What changes is the tense — and with it, what each question is reaching for.

Did it go well?

Memory is subject to the same negativity bias as present perception. Periods of a life that were mostly good are remembered through their failures. Relationships that were mostly nourishing are remembered through their damage. The first question asks the past to be seen whole — before examining what went wrong, examine what went right.

Did it truly matter?

Not everything that went wrong in the past deserves continued attention. Old slights, minor failures, embarrassments that felt enormous at the time — much of what the mind replays in the small hours carries no genuine consequence for how you now live. Past-tense discontinuation is about releasing what the mind returns to out of habit rather than necessity. When the answer is no, the path is discontinuation: let it go, and recover the attention it has been consuming.

Is it in my control to change?

In the past tense, this question cannot ask whether you can undo what happened. It asks whether any form of agency still remains: an apology not yet made, a relationship that could still be repaired, a reckoning that has been avoided but is still possible. When agency remains, the path is agency — directed not at changing the past, which is fixed, but at what the past has left open. When no agency remains, the path is acceptance. What cannot be undone can at least stop being fought.

The Future

What has not yet happened, and how should I enter it?

The future requires a different sequence. There is no condition yet to assess, no past to carry. The question is how to decide well before committing to what will become the case.

How will this affect the five dimensions?

Before asking whether something matters, see what it would actually do to your life. A decision examined in the abstract — a job offer, a move, a commitment — often looks different once its effects across the five dimensions are made concrete. Financial well-being may improve while connections strain. Physical well-being may benefit while identity is complicated. Seeing the full shape of the tradeoffs before committing allows the choice to be honest.

Does this truly matter?

This question comes second because the answer depends on what the first question has revealed. Assessed in the abstract, a possibility may seem significant or trivial; assessed against its actual effects across your life, the picture often shifts. Something that seemed urgent may prove weightless. Something that seemed minor may prove more consequential than it first appeared. When the answer is no, the path is discontinuation.

How easy is it to reverse this if you change your mind?

Not all commitments are equal in their permanence. Some are highly reversible — you can try something, discover it is wrong for you, and exit with relatively little cost. Others are not: a child, a marriage, a career, a financial commitment that would take years to unwind, a move to a place where you have no other roots. This question does not counsel against what is hard to reverse. It asks that you know, before committing, how much of your future freedom you are trading. A high-reversibility commitment can be entered on good evidence and revised if that evidence changes. A low-reversibility commitment requires greater certainty, because the cost of being wrong is higher and less recoverable.

When the Answer Is Unsure

Honest examination sometimes arrives at uncertainty. The uncertainty itself is information.

Is it going well? — Sometimes you cannot tell. The relationship is functional but not fulfilling. The career is stable but feels hollow. The body works but something is off. When you are unsure whether something is going well, the answer is usually that it is not — if it were going well, you would know. Look more specifically. Ask the question about a facet rather than the whole dimension, and the picture often sharpens.

Does it truly matter? — This is the question most often met with uncertainty. The two tests apply: would your life change if this disappeared? Is this concern actually yours? What truly matters tends to make itself known. What does not tends to fade once you stop feeding it attention.

Is it in my control? — Unsure here usually means partial control, which is addressed above. It can also mean you have not yet tested your agency — assuming you cannot change something because it has always been this way, or because past attempts failed. Before settling on acceptance, test the boundary. One honest attempt at change — a conversation, an application, a behavior shift — will tell you more about your actual control than extended reflection. There is also a subtler form of unsure: claiming you have no control because the alternative — having control and not yet exercising it — is harder to face.

Some things genuinely cannot be seen alone. If the questions consistently produce uncertainty no matter how specifically you ask them, the limitation may not be in the questions. A therapist, a trusted friend, someone who can observe what you cannot — these work alongside the mirror.

The Questions Together

For the present: Is it going well? If yes, appreciation. If no — does it truly matter? If no, discontinuation. If yes — is it in my control to change? If yes, agency. If no, acceptance.

For the past: the same questions, in the same sequence, in past tense. Did it go well? If yes, appreciation. If no — did it truly matter? If no, discontinuation. If yes — is it in my control to change? If yes, agency directed at what the past has left open. If no, acceptance of what is permanently settled.

For the future: a different sequence. How will this affect the five dimensions? Then — does this truly matter? Then — how easy is it to reverse? The answers produce discontinuation, agency, or acceptance.

The questions do the work of seeing. The work of living belongs to you.

IV.

The Five Dimensions

The question sets need somewhere to point. Applied without structure — to whatever happens to occupy attention at a given moment — they will miss what matters. The five dimensions provide that structure: a map of everything a human life contains, fixed across time, so the questions can be applied systematically within it.

Every human life, regardless of era, culture, or circumstances, can be understood through five dimensions:

> *Physical well-being — your body, its capacity, and its limits. This dimension covers how you sleep, how you move, how you manage pain, how you age, and what you put into your body.*

> *Emotional well-being — your inner world. This dimension covers your feelings, your mental health, the patterns of thought that shape your experience, and the ongoing quality of your inner life.*

Financial well-being — *your material resources and the freedom or constraint they create. This dimension covers your income, your expenses, your debts, your savings, your financial behavior, and the relationship between your material reality and the rest of your life.*

Connections — *the people in your life and how those relationships function. This dimension covers your intimate partnerships, your family, your friendships, your community, and the broader web of relationships that sustain or drain you. Loneliness is as much a part of this dimension as love.*

Identity — *who you are. This dimension covers your values, your sense of self, your relationship with purpose and meaning, and the ongoing question of whether the life you are living aligns with the person you take yourself to be. Identity's problems tend not to stay contained — they leak into every other dimension, which is why it is often the last place people look and the first place the trouble lives.*

Every experience you have — every source of ease or strain — traces to a root in one of these five. The dimensions are distinct at the level of sources, though they interact constantly: a problem in one can produce symptoms in several others.

Facets

Each dimension is too broad for the questions to be asked at its level. "Is my physical well-being going well?" does not produce an actionable answer, because physical well-being includes energy, fitness, chronic conditions, and more — some of which may be going well while others are not.

The questions operate at the level of facets. A facet is a specific part of a dimension — narrow enough that the questions produce a clear answer. "Is my energy going well?" is answerable.

The facets covered here were chosen because they are common, consequential, and illustrative. The pattern they teach holds for any facet the book does not name.

Finding the Right Facet

The dimension chapters name specific facets, and if your situation maps onto one of them, the questions are straightforward to apply. But life rarely arrives prelabeled. You may feel a general unease without being able to name what it is.

When the picture is blurry, start with the feeling and work backward. What, specifically, is bothering you? If it is dread on

Sunday evenings, you may be in the financial dimension if the dread is about work as income, or in the identity dimension if it is about work as meaning. If it is loneliness despite being surrounded by people, you may be in connections — or in identity, where something about your relationship with yourself is unresolved.

The level of specificity matters. "My finances are a mess" is too broad. "I earn enough but spend more than I make" is a facet — financial behavior. "I earn enough and save well but feel anxious about money constantly" is a different facet — the emotional dimension with a financial trigger. The narrower the target, the more useful the questions become.

If you cannot narrow it, read through the facets in the dimension chapters and notice where your attention catches. The facet that produces the strongest reaction — recognition, resistance, or discomfort — is usually the place to start.

Finding the Source

When something is wrong in your life, you feel it — but locating the source takes work. A problem may produce symptoms across several dimensions while its source belongs to only one. Loneliness that persists among people who care about you is not a connections problem — something in identity, in your relationship with yourself, is unresolved. Exhaustion that traces back to a career with no meaning is not a physical problem. The source lives somewhere specific, and the mirror gives different answers depending on where you point it.

Certain interactions are common enough to name. Physical depletion frequently cascades into emotional strain, and financial stress tends to erode connections. Identity confusion often disrupts more broadly — affecting emotions, habits, finances, and relationships at once — and the loss of connection can feed back into identity, because so much of who you are is formed and confirmed in relation to others. When the source is hard to find, these patterns are the first places to look.

When multiple dimensions are failing simultaneously, ask which one is holding the others hostage. In most cascades there is a root — find it and start there. If you cannot find it, start with the body: sleep, movement, and nutrition can be changed quickly, and small physical improvements create capacity for everything else.

If the body is not the root, look for the dimension where a single change would relieve the most pressure elsewhere: a financial decision that would reduce anxiety and ease a strained relationship, a conversation that would resolve the tension keeping you from sleep. The one thread, when pulled, that loosens the rest.

Two Cases

A man in his fifties notices he has been withdrawing from friends. He assumes the problem is social — he has become less interested, less willing to make plans — and decides to push harder. But when he examines the other dimensions, a pattern emerges. His sleep has deteriorated. His energy is lower. He has been relying on caffeine to get through afternoons and alcohol to wind down at night. The withdrawal is not a social problem. It is a physical one — his body is running on fumes, and social life is the first thing it sheds when energy becomes scarce.

The questions, applied to the right facet — energy — give him a clear answer. Is it going well? No. Does it truly matter? Yes. Is it in his control? Yes — the sleep, the caffeine cycle, the evening drinking are behavioral and reversible. The path is agency. Without tracing the source, he might have spent months pushing himself to be more social while the depletion continued.

A woman in her thirties spends every Sunday evening anxious about a colleague who seems to dislike her. The anxiety is real — she feels it. But the second question stops her. Does it truly matter? The colleague has no authority over her work. Their paths rarely cross. The dislike, even if real, carries no consequence. The path is discontinuation. The anxiety was consuming attention that her life needed elsewhere.

What the Mirror Produces

The simplest case is one facet, one path. You examine a specific part of your life and the questions produce a single clear answer.

More often, a situation contains several facets leading in different directions. You break it apart and ask the questions about each piece. The same experience can produce appreciation for what it gave, agency for what remains open, and acceptance for what is permanently settled — each clear once the pieces are separated.

Sometimes two dimensions produce answers that conflict. A promotion offers financial agency but threatens the connections that matter most to you. The mirror shows both answers with equal clarity and leaves the choice to you, because the relative weight of dimensions is personal. What it does is make the tradeoff visible and precise, so that the choosing is honest.

The answers are current readings, open to revision. What is beyond your control today may be within it tomorrow. What truly mattered last year may carry less weight now.

PART II:

THE DIMENSIONS

V.

Physical Well-Being

You have a body. It is the one thing you have carried since the beginning and will carry to the end. It carries you, sustains you, limits you, and — when it is working well — disappears from your attention, letting you focus on everything else that makes up a life. When it is not working well, nothing else works quite right either. Your thinking dulls, your patience thins, your capacity for other people shrinks, and tasks that were once automatic begin to require effort. Physical well-being is what the other four dimensions rest on.

Energy

Energy is your body's daily capacity — how much you have, how quickly it drains, how fully it returns. It is shaped by sleep, nutrition, hormonal health, stress, and underlying conditions. Of all the facets of physical well-being, energy is the one most people misread, because low energy normalizes slowly. You adjust your expectations downward. You compensate with caffeine, with willpower, with narrowed ambitions. You forget what it felt like to have more, and the diminished state begins to feel like who you are rather than what is happening to your body.

Energy is also the facet that reaches farthest into the rest of your life. When your energy is full, you say yes — to plans, to people, to challenges, to the difficult conversations and ambitious projects that require something extra. When it is depleted, you contract. You cancel, you postpone, you choose the easiest option — your body is rationing what little it has.

[C0501] David is fifty-three and runs a small landscaping business. His energy shows up reliably — enough to get through the day, enough left at the end for the people he cares about, enough that he rarely thinks about it. He does not think of his energy as a gift. That is exactly the condition appreciation is designed to address: the good that has become invisible because it has never been absent. Is his energy going well? Yes. The path is appreciation.

[C0502] Carmen is forty-four, and her energy collapsed over the course of six months. She used to be the person who got things done — reliable, present, always moving. Now she drags through the morning, hits a wall by early afternoon, and falls asleep on the couch most evenings before nine. She told herself it was stress, told herself she was getting older, and pushed through, because pushing through had always worked before.

When she holds up the mirror and looks at what changed, three things surface. Six months ago she took on a new role with earlier hours. To compensate for losing her evenings, she started staying up later — the only quiet time she had — cutting her sleep from seven hours to about five and a half. She replaced breakfast with coffee — sometimes three cups before noon — enough to mask the exhaustion until midday, when the caffeine wore off and the crash arrived. And she stopped her evening walks, which had been the one habit quietly regulating both her stress and her sleep for years.

None of these changes felt significant when they happened. Together, they dismantled her energy.

The questions: Is her energy going well? No — it has dropped significantly, and the decline is affecting her work, her mood, and her ability to be present for the people she cares about. Does it truly matter? Yes. This is not a manufactured concern; her daily functioning has deteriorated in ways she can feel and others can see. Is it in her control to change? Carmen assumed the answer was no — she assumed aging or stress were the cause, and neither felt fixable. The earlier hours are not in her control; the new role is not going away. But the behavioral responses to those hours are. The sleep debt she is running, the caffeine cycle she built to mask it, the walks she abandoned when her evenings disappeared — each of these is a decision she made without fully recognizing it, and each is reversible. The path is agency: the hours are fixed. The habits compounding their damage are hers to change.

Fitness and Movement

Fitness and movement is your body's ability to do what your life asks of it. Not athletic performance — functional capacity. Can you climb stairs without stopping, carry what needs carrying, get down on the floor and back up again, walk for thirty minutes without distress, sustain a day of physical activity without your body becoming the limiting factor? These are modest, functional benchmarks. They are the quiet markers of a body that cooperates with the life you are trying to live.

A body that moves well is one of the easiest things to take for granted. It is also the facet most distorted by external standards — the distance between functional fitness and the images presented by the fitness industry is vast, and many people who are perfectly healthy feel inadequate because they are measuring themselves against a standard that has nothing to do with how well their body actually serves them.

The person whose body works well enough for their life — who walks, climbs stairs, carries groceries, keeps up with their children — is often the last to recognize it as fitness. The path is appreciation.

For the person whose capacity has declined — who finds that the body can no longer do what the life asks of it without significant effort, or that recovery from exertion takes longer than it should — the path is agency. The specific acts are often unglamorous: more movement, less sedentary time, a physiotherapist, a consistent routine modest enough to sustain.

A different case: the body that is objectively performing well but that the person experiences as inadequate, measured against a standard with no relationship to how the body actually functions. Lifts tracked in a spreadsheet, body fat measured against images, a fitness that produces no satisfaction because the goal is a body measured against a comparison it was never designed to win. Is the fitness going well? Often yes. Does it truly matter — does the gap between current fitness and the pursued standard affect anything real? Usually not. The path is discontinuation of the standard. The movement stays.

Pain and Chronic Conditions

When your body has a condition that demands ongoing attention, your relationship with the physical dimension changes fundamentally. The body is no longer background. It is foreground, every day, requiring management, negotiation, and decisions that people without the condition never have to make.

This facet covers a wide territory: chronic pain in its many forms — back, joints, migraines, nerve damage, fibromyalgia; chronic illness — diabetes, heart disease, autoimmune disorders, cancer; disability, whether present from birth or acquired through injury or disease; and acute conditions that leave lasting effects, such as strokes, surgeries, or injuries that do not fully heal.

[C0503] Alan is forty-six and, by every objective measure, healthy. His most recent physical was unremarkable — blood pressure normal, cholesterol within range, no findings of concern. His doctor told him he was in good shape.

Alan feels fragile. Every headache triggers a quiet spiral of worry about what it might mean. Every unfamiliar sensation in his chest sends him searching for explanations online. Every new mole, every muscle twitch, every moment of unexplained fatigue becomes a potential catastrophe. He has been to the emergency room twice in the past year for symptoms that turned out to be driven by anxiety — chest tightness that was a panic response, abdominal pain produced by stress.

His body is fine. His experience of his body is the problem.

The questions, applied to his body: Is it going well? By every clinical measure, yes. His body needs no treatment. The path for his physical health is appreciation — a body doing exactly what it should, confirmed repeatedly by doctors, with no genuine findings of concern. The questions applied to his health anxiety produce a different answer. Is the anxiety going well? No — it is driving emergency room visits, sleepless nights, and a persistent experience of his body as threatening rather than functional. Does it truly matter? Yes — it is affecting his quality of life, his sleep, and his daily experience of being alive. Is it in his control to change? The anxiety is real, and it has a home: not in the physical dimension, which has nothing wrong in it, but in the emotional dimension, where the fear, the scanning, and the catastrophizing can be examined in their own right.

But the mirror also shows something the body examination alone would miss. Alan can articulate that his body is fine. He has heard it from three doctors. And the next time his chest tightens, he will be back on the internet at two in the morning. The recognition is there. The release lags behind — and the inability to release a fear he knows is unfounded is itself the signal. That signal does not live in the physical dimension. The real work is in the emotional dimension, where the anxiety is the subject of examination rather than an afterthought — and where the questions will produce a clear answer. Is the anxiety going well? No. Does it truly matter? Yes. Is it in his control to change? That is what the examination in the emotional dimension is for — and until it is done, the path cannot be named. What it will not be is appreciation. What it will not be is discontinuation. The path will be agency, or acceptance, or both across different facets of the anxiety — but that determination belongs to the examination that has not yet been done. The physical dimension has already given its answer: appreciation. The emotional dimension is where the real work begins.

[C0504] Frank is fifty-two and has lived with chronic pain for eleven years. The thing that changed his life was not the pain — it was the decision to stop organizing his life around the search for its elimination.

For the first five years after the pain became chronic, he treated it as a problem to solve. He tried everything: two surgeries, extensive physical therapy, chiropractic treatment, acupuncture, steroid injections, massage, several medications, yoga, meditation, an inversion table, and one clinical trial. Some of these helped at the margins — reduced the pain from unbearable to manageable, gave him a few better weeks, expanded his range of motion temporarily. None cured it. He spent tens of thousands of dollars. He organized his days around the search for relief — every new practitioner represented hope, every failed treatment a private despair. He became the person with the back problem, and the search for a fix became the center of his life.

After the second surgery failed to produce lasting improvement, his pain specialist said something Frank was not ready to hear: "This is your baseline. Let us build from here." He resisted that for another two years. Then, slowly, over months rather than in a single moment, he stopped resisting.

The questions, applied to where Frank is now: Is it going well? No. He lives with daily pain that limits his activity, disrupts his sleep, and shapes every decision he makes. Does it truly matter? Yes — it affects every part of his life. Is it in his control to change? He has tried everything reasonable. Some things helped manage the pain; nothing eliminated it. The remaining pain — the baseline — is not in his control. The path is acceptance.

But here is what acceptance looks like in practice, and why it looks like defeat from the outside and is something else entirely. Frank still manages the pain — the stretching, the pacing, the heat packs, the medication that takes the edge off. These are all agency within the limitation. What he released was the search itself: the cycle of hope and disappointment, the belief that the right treatment was still out there, the organizing principle that kept his entire life oriented toward a cure that would never come.

Acceptance, for Frank, redirected the work. Within the baseline he did not choose, there is still a life to tend: his work, which he has adapted to accommodate his limits; his relationships, which existed before the pain and continue through it; the things that bring him satisfaction that do not require the range of motion the second surgery was supposed to restore. He is not the person he was at forty-one, the year the pain began. He is something the person at forty-one could not have imagined: someone who has organized a life inside a limitation and finds it, against all expectation, sufficient. That is one of the hardest forms of appreciation in the physical dimension — seeing clearly what is present rather than measuring what is absent.

Substances and Nutrition

What you put into your body — and what you rely on — shapes your physical well-being in ways that are often invisible until they become undeniable. The question is not whether your nutrition is ideal. The question is whether it is going well.

Substance use follows the same logic. A glass of wine with dinner is different from a glass you need to get through the evening. The line between use and dependence is not always obvious from the inside, and the questions help draw it.

The person who has made peace with a substance — who no longer drinks, who no longer smokes, who moved from dependence to ease — is often carrying something worth naming: not just abstinence but the clarity of a choice made and held. The path is appreciation, and the risk is the same as in every appreciation case: taking the settled state for granted and forgetting what it cost to reach it. The person still in the pattern — who drinks every evening and has known for years that this is a problem, who continues not because they cannot see the picture but because the dependency has made the first step feel enormous — already knows the answer to the first two questions. The work is the third: what is within reach, what is one concrete action, and what help would make that action possible. The path is agency, and it is often a smaller act than the person imagines — one call, one conversation, one appointment.

Nutrition follows the same structure. The relevant question is not whether your diet matches a published standard but whether what you eat supports your energy, your health, and your daily function. Weight, when the mirror reaches it, is one of the facets most susceptible to the wrong object. The person who has been measuring their body against an external standard — a number on a scale, an image absorbed from culture, a comparison that has nothing to do with how well the body actually functions — often finds, when the questions are applied honestly, that the body is fine. The standard is not. The path is discontinuation of the wrong standard — discontinuation of a measurement that has been producing effort and guilt without producing the only thing that actually matters: a body that works.

Body Image and Aging

Body image is deeper than vanity. Your relationship with the physical form you inhabit gets shaped early — by family, by culture, by the messages you absorbed about what a body should look like. The gap between how your body actually functions and how you feel about it can be wide, and it is the gap that needs examination.

[C0505] Lorraine is fifty-two and has been trying to lose thirty pounds for most of her adult life. She has tried diets, programs, calorie counting, structured exercise, and, at one point, a medically supervised protocol. She has lost the weight twice and gained it back both times. The effort has consumed years. She is a competent, active woman who climbs stairs, walks miles, and has no conditions her doctors consider a problem. Her body functions well by every clinical measure. The dissatisfaction has been running so long it has become invisible — the water she swims in rather than a condition she is in.

The questions, applied to the inherited standard she has been measuring herself against: Is it going well? No — three decades of effort, guilt, and self-reproach without producing anything else. Does it truly matter? Her body functions well. It supports her life. The standard it fails to meet is one assembled from sources with no interest in whether she can live her life well. Does the gap between her body and that standard truly matter? No. Is it in her control to change? Yes — not the body, necessarily, but the standard. The path is discontinuation of a measurement she has been applying to herself for thirty years without ever questioning whether it was hers to apply — not of attention to health, which belongs, but of the standard itself.

The relief this produces is the feeling of a burden set down — not a problem solved — the recognition that the effort was never going to produce the satisfaction she was looking for, because the standard was wrong, not the body.

Aging changes the terms of every other facet. The body at fifty differs from the body at thirty — strength, recovery, appearance, hormonal balance, the things that happen without effort. These changes are not illness, but they are real, and the moment when you notice them and have not yet adjusted is exactly what the mirror is for. Something has shifted. The path is agency: to examine the change honestly and decide what to do with what is actually there.

Other Facets

Other facets of physical well-being include sleep, which is both a facet in its own right and the foundation everything else is built on — its disruption reaches into energy, cognition, mood, and immunity in ways that few other physical variables can; sexual health, including changes in desire, function, comfort, and confidence that belong in the same honest examination as any other physical facet; and dental health. Sensory changes such as declining vision or hearing alter daily function and often go unaddressed longer than they should. Recovery from surgery or acute illness, the effects of long-term medication on daily functioning, preventive care and the ongoing relationship with the medical system, and reproductive health including fertility — each can be examined with the same questions.

The Past: What Happened in This Dimension, and How Should I Carry It?

The body accumulates history in ways that are uniquely physical. You carry the consequences of how you lived — the years of neglect or discipline, the choices made before you understood their cost, the events that altered what your body can and cannot do. The past question set applied to the physical dimension asks what happened, whether it mattered, and whether anything remains open.

[C0506] Dennis is fifty-eight and his cardiologist delivered a verdict three years ago that he had been quietly expecting. Mild coronary artery disease. Nothing requiring immediate intervention, but a finding with a clear history behind it: twenty years of heavy smoking, ended a decade ago; a sustained stretch in his forties when he ate badly, moved rarely, and drank more than he acknowledged; a decade of moderate overweight that his annual physicals noted and he disregarded. He stopped smoking. He did not stop much else. The disease his cardiologist is now managing is, in a traceable line, the result of how he lived between thirty-five and fifty.

He does not say this to punish himself. He says it because it is true, and because he spent some time, after the diagnosis, trying to tell himself it was not. Bad luck, he told himself.

Genetics. His father had heart disease. The argument felt persuasive for a few months and then hollow — because he knew, more specifically than the argument required, exactly what he had done and not done for fifteen years.

The mirror applied to the past: Did it go well? No. The choices he made over those years contributed directly to a condition he is now managing for life. Did it truly matter? Yes — the consequences are real, permanent in degree, and present every day in the medications he takes, the exertion levels he monitors, the procedures that may still be ahead. Is there anything in his control to change? He cannot unlive those years. The disease exists. But the past has left several things open. His current habits are within reach: he exercises now with cardiac supervision, eats differently, sleeps adequately, manages stress in ways he did not bother to before. These are not undoing what happened — they are agency applied to what the past left open.

What he has released — slowly, not cleanly — is the argument with the past itself. The years he spent telling himself it would not catch up with him, and then the months after the diagnosis spent telling himself it was not really his fault. Both were versions of the same refusal: to see clearly what happened and carry it as it was, rather than as he wished it had been. The past requires acceptance. What it left open — the habits, the management, the choices still available — is agency.

[C0507] Nina is forty-one and was treated for breast cancer at thirty-four. The treatment was brutal and the outcome was good — complete remission, confirmed through seven years of follow-up with no recurrence. Her oncologist considers her cured by any reasonable clinical definition. Her body, which bore the treatment and came through it, is healthy.

She still introduces herself, in certain contexts, as a cancer survivor. She still organizes her relationship with her body around the illness — monitoring symptoms with a vigilance that her doctors consider disproportionate to her current risk, declining physical commitments because she is not sure what her body can handle, holding herself at a slight distance from her own health as if full confidence in it might jinx something. The illness was seven years ago. The self-concept it produced is still running.

The mirror applied to the past: Did it go well? No — cancer at thirty-four, and the treatment required to address it, was genuinely terrible. Did it truly matter? Yes, entirely. Is there anything in her control to change? The illness cannot be undone, and what it cost her — physically and otherwise — cannot be recovered. The path for the cancer itself is acceptance: it happened, it was real, and no examination changes that.

But the past and the present are not the same question. The illness is past and requires acceptance. The identity she built around it is present and requires a different examination — and that examination belongs not in the physical dimension but in identity, where self-concept lives. The cancer survivor who organized her body-relationship around an active illness, and who has not updated that organization in seven years of evidence that the illness is gone, is carrying a self-concept that no longer matches her body. The past produced the identity. The present is where the identity now lives, and where it can be examined on its own terms: is the self-concept going well? No — it is organized around an illness that is gone. Does it truly matter? Yes — the outdated organization is constraining her relationship with her own body. Is it in her control to change? Yes. The path is discontinuation of the cancer survivor identity as the organizing principle of her body-relationship, and agency in building a self-concept that matches the seven years of evidence she has actually accumulated.

The Future: What Has Not Yet Happened, and How Should I Enter It?

How will this affect the five dimensions? Does this truly matter? How easy is it to reverse if I change my mind?

Physical commitments affect everything else. To treat the body differently, to demand more of it, or to alter it permanently is to change the instrument through which every other dimension is experienced. The future question set applied to the physical dimension asks you to see those effects clearly before committing.

[C0508] Marcus is forty-six and wants to run a marathon. Not to prove something, or so he tells himself — but he is not entirely sure that is true, and the honesty is worth something. He ran competitively in college and has done nothing close to it since. He is fit in a general sense, active, without any conditions that would prevent training. The goal is real. The question is whether entering it is wise.

How will this affect the five dimensions? Physically, training for a marathon at forty-six is demanding — the mileage required, the recovery time, the injury risk that rises with age and with going from moderate fitness to high-volume training quickly. His schedule, already full, would compress further; the training would take time that currently belongs to other things. Financially, the commitment is modest. His marriage would feel the time pressure. Emotionally, there is something in this goal that matters to him — a reconnection with a version of himself that predates the decades of desk work — and that belongs in the picture too.

Does it truly matter? When he examines it honestly, yes — what the training would give him: a physical project with clear structure, a reason to use his body seriously, something that requires him rather than just his capacity to sit still and think.

How easy is it to reverse? Highly. He can begin training, discover it is wrong for him — the injuries, the time, the toll on other things — and stop. No permanent commitment has been made. The cost of being wrong is a few months of effort.

The path is agency — the examination is complete, the tradeoffs are visible, and what remains is the decision.

[C0509] Susan is fifty-one and has been thinking about a knee replacement for two years. The arthritis in her left knee is real and has been confirmed by imaging — bone-on-bone in the medial compartment, a condition that will not improve on its own and that her orthopedic surgeon considers surgical. The pain is manageable most days with anti-inflammatories and activity modification, but it limits her: stairs are slow, walking distances that used to be effortless now require planning, the hiking she has done most of her adult life has mostly stopped.

The surgery her surgeon recommends would, by most accounts, resolve the pain and restore significant function. The outcomes for knee replacement at her age are generally good. She knows all of this. She has known it for two years. She has not scheduled the surgery.

How will this affect the five dimensions? The surgery would, if successful, restore physical capacity she has lost — a genuine gain in the physical dimension and, by extension, in the emotional and connections dimensions that depend on her ability to move through the world. The recovery is real: six weeks of significant limitation, months of rehabilitation, a period of dependence on other people that she finds difficult to contemplate. Financially, it is manageable.

Does it truly matter? Yes — the knee is affecting her daily life, her mood, and the activities that give her life texture.

How easy is it to reverse? A knee replacement is not reversible. The joint that exists now will not exist after the surgery. If the outcome is poor — persistent pain, limited function, complications — the path back does not exist. After surgery, the question will no longer be about the original knee. It will be about the artificial one, with whatever it provides and whatever it costs.

This is the case where the third question governs. The surgery may well be the right decision. But its irreversibility means that the certainty required before committing is higher than for a decision she could undo. Two years of delay is, in part, the appropriate weight being given to a permanent change. What the mirror asks her is whether she has examined it honestly enough to know. Has she spoken with others who have undergone the surgery, not just her surgeon? Has she tried the nonsurgical management her surgeon offered and found it insufficient, or has she avoided the question by avoiding both the surgery and the alternatives? If the answer to the third question is that she has not yet done the examination the decision requires, the path is not yet agency. It is the agency of completing that examination — so that when she commits, she commits with the clarity the decision's permanence demands.

The body is the most concrete of the five dimensions and, in some ways, the most honest. It does not pretend. It simply does what it can with what it has been given, and shows you, with varying degrees of bluntness, what that is. The next dimension has no such candor. What you feel is real — but where it comes from, and what it means, requires a different kind of looking.

VI.

Emotional Well-Being

The physical dimension lives in the body — visible, measurable, concrete. This one lives in the quality of your inner experience.

You have an inner life. It is always running — a continuous stream of feelings, reactions, interpretations, and moods that color everything you experience. When your inner life is settled, the world looks manageable. When it falters, the same world looks threatening, exhausting, or empty. Emotional well-being is the steadiness or turbulence of your moods, your capacity to experience both pleasure and pain without being overwhelmed by either. It includes the quality of your inner dialogue — whether it runs roughly kind or persistently harsh.

This dimension requires a distinction the physical chapter could skip: emotions can originate somewhere else. When you feel anxious about money, the anxiety is real, but if it disappears the moment your financial situation improves, the source was financial, not emotional. When you feel angry at your partner, the anger is real, but if it traces back to exhaustion, the source is physical. The emotion was the messenger, not the message. The questions produce different answers depending on where the source lives, so this chapter focuses on emotions whose source is emotional — feelings and patterns that persist even when your health, finances, relationships, and sense of self are intact.

Peacefulness and Contentment

A quiet sense of ease. Not euphoria, but a general feeling that your life, taken as a whole, is all right. You wake most mornings without dread. You move through your days without a persistent sense that something is wrong. You have worries and frustrations like anyone, but these pass through rather than define the texture of your experience. The hum of your inner life is calm rather than agitated.

Peacefulness arrives quietly. It demands nothing the way anxiety or anger or sadness does. It is the emotional equivalent of the body that works — present, valuable, invisible until it is gone. Those who have it rarely recognize it. Those who have lost it usually did not notice it leaving.

[C0601] Martin is forty-two and is not sure whether he is all right. This is a different situation from knowing something is wrong. He feels neither bad nor good — a low-level flatness that he cannot decide whether to worry about or ignore. Some weeks it lifts and he thinks he was making too much of it. Other weeks it settles in and he wonders whether this is what the beginning of something looks like.

Is it going well? Martin's answer: I don't know.

When Martin narrows the question — Is my sleep going well? Yes. Is my marriage going well? Yes. Is my sense of purpose going well? — he pauses. He was promoted eighteen months ago into a management role he never sought and actively dislikes. The flatness coincides almost exactly with the promotion.

The unsure resolves. His emotional well-being is not going well, and the source is not emotional — it is in the identity dimension, in a role that chafes. The vagueness of the feeling was a product of looking at the wrong level. Once he narrowed the question, the picture sharpened. The source is real, it matters, and it is in his control to change. The path is agency, located in the identity dimension where the source lives: whether he can return to the individual contributor work he was promoted out of, move laterally into a role that uses his skills without requiring the management he dislikes, or restructure his current role to reduce what he finds most draining. Any of these is agency. The path is agency.

[C0602] Vera is thirty-six and used to be at ease. She remembers it — not as a distant memory but as something she can almost still feel, like warmth that has recently left a room. For most of her twenties and into her early thirties, her inner life was calm. She handled stress well, recovered from setbacks quickly, and generally felt that things would work out.

Over the past two years, that has changed. She feels tense most of the time now, even when nothing specific is wrong. She sleeps less soundly. Her patience is shorter. She finds herself snapping at people she cares about and then feeling guilty about it afterward. She feels like a stranger in her own skin, and the cause eludes her.

When she looks carefully at what changed, a pattern emerges — a series of small decisions that felt, each time, like adjustments rather than losses. A new role at work, intellectually engaging but isolating: she works alone most of the day, and the casual social contact that used to texture her routine quietly disappeared. Her evenings, once unstructured, filled with the phone — scrolling, reading the news, absorbing content that reliably left her feeling worse than when she started. A journaling habit, sporadic but real, that she stopped because the new role was demanding and something had to give — and that she now recognizes, too late, as the way she had been clearing what accumulated during her days. The weekends, scheduled to capacity out of guilt and obligation, until there was no unstructured time left. None of it felt significant. Together it dismantled the conditions that had kept her settled.

Is her emotional well-being going well? No — the contentment she used to have has been replaced by a persistent tension that she feels daily. Does it truly matter? Yes. It is affecting her relationships, her sleep, and her overall quality of life. Is it in her control to change? When she traces the erosion to its sources, she finds that each one is addressable. The isolation at work can be partially offset; the evenings reclaimed from the phone, the journaling resumed, the weekends pared back. The path is agency — a series of small restorations, rebuilding the conditions that supported her contentment before she unknowingly dismantled them.

Gratitude

Gratitude is the capacity to notice what is good — a genuine orientation toward the actual texture of your life, not a performance. Seeing what is already present, without distortion, and registering its value. This is distinct from optimism, which bends toward the future.

Gratitude can coexist with difficulty. A person can be genuinely grateful for a life that contains real pain, real loss, and real limitation — the life, taken whole, contains enough goodness to be worth recognizing. This is the refusal to let what is hard erase everything else.

[C0603] Oscar is fifty-eight and rebuilt his life after his business partner of fourteen years embezzled from their company. The fraud was systematic, concealed over several years, and when it was discovered, it nearly destroyed the business Oscar had spent his career building. He spent two years in litigation. The case was settled out of court for an amount that did not come close to what was taken. The partner received no criminal charges. He lives, as far as Oscar knows, without consequence.

In the years since, Oscar rebuilt. The business survived, smaller than before. His marriage strengthened under pressure rather than breaking. His two children, who watched their father navigate a betrayal without becoming someone he was not, are close to him in a way he values above almost everything else. He has made new friendships. He has found that the life on the other side of the worst thing that happened to him is genuinely good.

He is also still angry. Not in a consuming way — the anger does not run his days. But it is there, quiet and permanent, in the part of him that knows what was taken and that no accounting was ever made. He has not resolved it because it cannot be resolved. There is no apology coming. There is only the fact of what happened and the life he has built regardless.

The questions applied to Oscar's gratitude: Is it going well? Yes — the rebuilt life is genuinely good, and he knows it. The path is appreciation. The questions applied to the anger: Is it going well? No — the wrong that produced it was real and was never adjudicated. Does it truly matter? Yes — it was a serious betrayal with permanent consequences. Is it in his control to change? The fraud cannot be undone. The partner will not be held accountable. What remains is unchangeable. The path is acceptance — acceptance of a permanent fact: no further expenditure of effort will produce the accounting he deserves.

Oscar holds both: gratitude for the life he has built, and acceptance of an anger that has no object left to address. Neither cancels the other. This is the full picture.

Anxiety

Anxiety is the inner alarm that fires without a proportionate threat. Everyone experiences it sometimes — a flutter before a presentation, a tightness before a difficult conversation, a restless night before an uncertain day. In proportionate doses, it is useful. It sharpens attention, prepares you, and signals that something matters.

The anxiety this facet examines has outgrown its usefulness — the kind that operates without a clear cause, or with a cause so disproportionate to the response that the alarm is doing more harm than the thing it is sounding for. A financial crisis or a health scare can produce fear that resembles this pattern, but its source is in another dimension. The anxiety examined here lives in the emotional dimension itself, independent of external circumstances — a pattern that precedes the events, rather than a response to them.

[C0604] Grace is thirty-seven and has lived with anxiety for as long as she can remember. She has tried to change it. She has been in therapy twice — it helped with specific coping strategies but left the underlying tendency intact. She takes medication that reduces the peaks without touching the baseline. She exercises, meditates, limits caffeine, and does everything the literature suggests. The anxiety is better managed than it has ever been. It remains, and her therapist has gently suggested it may never fully go.

Is her anxiety going well? No — it is a permanent feature of her inner life that she would prefer not to have. Does it truly matter? Yes — it affects her daily experience, her energy, and her capacity for ease. Is it in her control to change? She has exercised every form of agency available to her, and the results have been meaningful but partial. The anxiety that remains, after all the management, appears to be constitutional — part of her neurological wiring rather than a pattern she can unlearn. The path is acceptance. Not acceptance of suffering — the management continues, and it helps. But acceptance that this is her version of a settled inner life: the earned calm of someone who has done the work, rather than the calm that comes from an absence of anxiety, but the calm that comes from knowing how to live alongside it.

[C0605] Evelyn is forty-three and remembers when anxiety ran her life. For most of her twenties and thirties, she lived with a constant undercurrent of dread — a feeling that something bad was about to happen, though she could never say what. She worried about her health, her relationships, her career, her family, the future, the past. The worry moved from target to target; when one concern was resolved, another took its place, as if the anxiety needed an object and would find one regardless of the facts.

At thirty-five, she began working with a therapist. The work was slow, undramatic, and effective. Over the course of several years, she learned to recognize the anxiety as a pattern rather than a series of legitimate alarms. She did not eliminate it — it still surfaces, particularly during times of stress — but she changed her relationship with it. It no longer runs her days. It arrives, she notices it, and most of the time it passes without requiring action.

Is her emotional well-being going well? Yes. She has done the work, the pattern has shifted, and her daily experience has improved significantly. The path is appreciation — not for the anxiety, which she would happily live without, but for the stability she has built. The current calm did not arrive on its own. It was earned through years of therapy, through the slow practice of recognizing anxious thoughts as patterns rather than alarms, through the behavioral guardrails — the sleep, the reduced alcohol, the limits on catastrophic news — that she maintains because she knows what happens without them. What she has is the presence of practices that keep the anxiety from running her days, and those practices require ongoing attention. The path is appreciation: see what is working, and protect it.

Emotional Regulation

Your ability to experience emotions without being overtaken by them is a quiet but essential part of emotional well-being. Regulation means the capacity to feel anger without being consumed by it, to feel sadness without spiraling, to sit with discomfort without immediately reaching for an escape. For many people, regulation can be learned and improved, making this one of the richest facets of agency within emotional well-being.

The person who is dysregulated knows it — she has said things she regrets, recovered from small provocations at a cost she can feel, noticed that managing her own reactions is a tax she pays continuously. The path is agency, and it is one of the most available forms of agency in the emotional dimension. The capacity to regulate can be developed through therapy, through mindfulness practice, through the slow and unglamorous work of noticing reactions slightly sooner each time. The improvement is not dramatic — a person who was always about to overflow becomes someone who occasionally tips over and recovers faster than they used to. Compounded across years, a slightly longer pause between impulse and response changes what a life feels like from the inside.

Is regulation going well — are you moving through difficult moments without the cost running your days? The path is appreciation: what works here requires the same protection as anything else that works. The practices that produce it require maintenance; when they stop, the old threshold returns.

Is regulation not going well — do you hear the same regrets, pay the same tax, find yourself back at the same threshold? The path is agency. The capacity can be developed, the work is available, and the improvement — though unglamorous — compounds.

Regulation fluctuates more than most facets. A period of high stress can erode what years of practice built. The question is not only where you are but whether the direction is right.

Anger

Anger is the emotion that fires when something feels wrong — when a boundary has been crossed, an injustice has occurred, or a threat has been perceived. In its proportionate form, anger is useful. This facet examines your relationship with anger as an ongoing pattern: whether it arrives too quickly and burns too hot, or whether it lingers long past the moment that warranted it, draining energy that belongs elsewhere.

As with anxiety, the anger examined here has its source in the emotional dimension itself — a pattern that lives in you regardless of circumstances. If you are angry because your employer is exploiting you, the source is elsewhere and the work is there.

The person whose anger arrives too fast is running a pattern that outruns their intention to interrupt it. The anger is not a response to this particular slow driver or misplaced tool — it is a default that activates before assessment can occur. The path is agency: the pattern is learned, and learned patterns can be changed, though not easily and not alone.

The person whose anger lingers — old, proportionate, directed at something that cannot be undone — faces a different question. The anger is justified, and justification changes nothing about the energy it consumes. The path is acceptance: not releasing the anger, but ceasing to spend effort expecting it to produce a result it cannot produce.

Grief

Grief is the cost of having loved something real. It belongs in this chapter not because something is wrong when you grieve but because grief is one of the most significant emotional experiences a human being can have, and the mirror can help you navigate it.

Grief does not move through tidy stages. It arrives in waves — sometimes predictable, often not — and its intensity bears no reliable relationship to the passage of time. A person can function well for months and then be leveled by a song, a smell, a Tuesday afternoon that looks exactly like the last Tuesday they spent with the person who is gone.

[C0606] Margaret is sixty-eight. Her husband Richard died two years ago, after forty-one years of marriage. The first year was what she expected — difficult, disorienting, full of firsts she did not want: the first holiday alone, the first spring without him in the garden, the first time she reached for the phone to tell him something and remembered, mid-dial, that there was no one to call.

The second year surprised her. The grief changed shape. It did not diminish exactly — it became less a constant presence and more a visitor, arriving with intensity but no longer staying indefinitely. In the spaces between the visits, Margaret found something she did not expect: a genuine appreciation for what she and Richard had built. Not a sentimental, retrospective glow — a clear-eyed recognition that the marriage had been, taken whole, a remarkable thing. Imperfect, sometimes difficult, occasionally tedious — and deeply, fundamentally good.

Is her emotional well-being going well? This is a question that resists a simple answer. The grief itself is not going well — it is painful, and the first question, applied to the grief, says no. But the grief is about something — a marriage that was deeply, fundamentally good — and that something was going well for forty-one years. The appreciation lives there, in what the grief reveals about what was lost. The path is appreciation — not for the loss, which she would undo in an instant, but for what the loss reveals about what was there.

Depression

Depression is a sustained lowering of mood, energy, and capacity that persists beyond what circumstances explain. Everyone has bad weeks. Depression is something different — a condition in which the inner life dims. Pleasure fades, motivation drains, the future flattens into a colorless expanse that is difficult to care about. Sleep suffers, appetite shifts, concentration frays, and the ability to engage with the people and activities that once mattered recedes. Among the most common forms of emotional suffering, depression is also one of the most important facets to examine without evasion, because it distorts the very instrument — your capacity for honest self-assessment — that the question sets depend on.

This distortion is worth naming directly. Depression tells you that nothing is going well, that nothing matters, and that nothing is in your control. All three of these messages may be false, but they feel absolutely true from inside the experience. A depressed person applying the questions will often arrive at answers shaped by the depression itself rather than by the reality of their situation. This does not mean the mirror is useless for depression — but in active depression, the person applying it is often too close to the condition to apply it accurately. The mirror may need to be held by someone else first. A therapist, a doctor, a trusted person who can see what the depression has obscured.

[C0607] Lillian is fifty and has lived with depression for most of her adult life. She has been in treatment for twelve years — medication, therapy, and the ongoing management of a condition she has come to understand is constitutional rather than situational. She has tried multiple medications and found one that works well enough. She has a therapist she trusts. Her depression is not gone — it surfaces in predictable patterns, especially in winter, and she has learned to recognize the early signals and respond before it deepens.

Her life, around the depression, is functioning. Her work is steady. Her marriage has survived the hard years and is now genuinely good — her husband understands the condition and does not try to fix it, which is one of the most valuable things a partner can do. Her relationship with her two adult children is close. She exercises regularly, not because she enjoys it during depressive episodes but because she has learned, through years of evidence, that it shortens them.

Is her emotional well-being going well? Yes — not in the sense that the depression is absent, but in the sense that it is managed. The treatment is working. The episodes are shorter and less severe than they were a decade ago. The architecture she has built around the condition — the medication, the therapy, the exercise, the partner who understands, the self-awareness that lets her catch an episode early — is holding. The path is appreciation — appreciation of the management — the architecture she built, not the condition it contains. What Lillian has built is a life that works despite the condition, and that is worth seeing clearly and protecting deliberately. Any change to the architecture — stopping medication because she feels fine, skipping therapy because it seems unnecessary, abandoning the exercise — risks destabilizing something that took years to build. The path is appreciation: see it, name it, and protect it.

[C0608] Phillip is forty-one and has been depressed for two years without treatment. He knows something is wrong. He has less energy than he used to. He has withdrawn from friends. He drinks more in the evenings. His work performance has declined — enough that he has noticed, and he suspects his manager has too. He sleeps poorly, wakes early, and lies in bed with a weight on his chest that he cannot name.

He has not sought help. Not because he does not believe in therapy — he has no objection to it in principle. He has not sought help because the depression itself has eroded his motivation to address it. This is one of depression's most difficult features: it disables the very capacity — initiative, energy, and the hope that things could be different — that seeking treatment requires. He tells himself he will make an appointment next week. Next week arrives and he does not.

Is his emotional well-being going well? No — two years of sustained, progressive decline. Does it truly matter? Yes — it is affecting his work, his relationships, his health, and his daily experience of being alive. Is it in his control to change? The answer must be direct. Yes. He did not choose the depression and cannot will it away. Treatment is within his control. The path is agency: one phone call, one doctor, the beginning of a process he has been putting off. Depression makes even small acts feel enormous, but the picture is honest. The help exists, it is accessible, and the only thing between Phillip and the start of treatment is the call he has not yet made.

[C0609] Hannah is forty-six and has treatment-resistant depression. She has tried four medications, two forms of therapy, exercise regimens, dietary changes, and a course of transcranial magnetic stimulation. Some of these helped moderately. None eliminated the baseline condition. Her psychiatrist describes her depression as chronic and partially treatment-responsive — the medication she is on now takes the edge off the worst episodes, but a low-grade heaviness persists most days, and she has come to understand that it may always persist.

Hannah's situation is the emotional equivalent of Frank's chronic pain. The condition is real, it is not going away, and the reasonable interventions have been attempted. Is her emotional well-being going well? No — the depression is a daily presence that affects her energy, her relationships, and her experience of living. Does it truly matter? Yes. Is it in her control to change? She has exhausted the agency available to her. New treatments may emerge — the field is advancing — and she remains open to trying them. But the current reality is that the depression, at its present level, is not something her effort can eliminate.

The path is acceptance. Hannah cannot will the depression away. She can build a life that accounts for it — a life with lower peaks and more rest, with relationships that understand the condition, with work that accommodates the bad days, with small pleasures that the depression has not fully erased. She can stop holding her life against a version of itself that does not exist. The depression is part of the picture. It is not the whole picture. And the parts of the picture it does not touch — her intelligence, her humor on good days, her love for her daughter, her ability to read and think and care about the world — are real and worth protecting. The path is acceptance: acceptance of the depression as something that is there, and that a life can be built around honestly.

Guilt

Guilt disguises itself as conscience, which makes it one of the most difficult emotional facets to examine clearly. A person carrying guilt feels, at some level, that the discomfort is deserved — that it is the correct response to something they did or failed to do, and that releasing it would be a moral failure.

Proportionate guilt: you did something real, the harm was genuine, and the guilt is a signal to make amends where amends are possible or to accept what cannot be undone. The path is agency — repair what you can — or acceptance — carry what you cannot repair without letting it consume what remains.

Disproportionate guilt: the guilt that attaches itself to things you did not cause, could not have prevented, or have already addressed. This guilt does not truly matter — the feelings are real. The path is discontinuation, and it is one of the hardest forms of discontinuation the emotional dimension contains, because letting go of guilt feels, to the person holding it, like letting go of responsibility itself.

Other Facets

Other facets of emotional well-being include suppressed anger, in which the emotion is buried so thoroughly that it no longer surfaces even when it would be proportionate; trauma and its lasting effects on the emotional baseline; and emotional numbness — the absence of feeling rather than the presence of pain, and no less worth examining. Forgiveness is an act — a choice — and when it is available the path is agency. The loss of positive experience — joy, curiosity, delight — whose fading can signal burnout or a life running too long in survival mode, belongs here too. So does loneliness as an emotional condition distinct from social isolation, and the relationship between emotional well-being and the stories you tell about your past, which shape the present more than most people examine. Each can be examined with the same questions.

The Past: What Happened in This Dimension, and How Should I Carry It?

Did it go well? Did it truly matter? Is there anything still in my control to change?

The emotional past is a record of how events were felt, processed — or not processed — and what residue they left behind. What you carry from the past in this dimension is often not the event itself but your relationship with it: a replay that continues after the productive examination has ended, a wound that no longer has an active source but still shapes how you move through the world, a grief that was set aside when circumstances demanded it and never fully faced.

The past question set applied to the emotional dimension asks whether what you are still carrying deserves the energy it consumes.

[C0610] James is fifty-seven. His father died when James was thirty-one, and James did not grieve him. He could not. His father died suddenly, in the middle of a period when James's own life was at maximum pressure: a young marriage, a new business, two small children. The death arrived, the funeral happened, and James returned to his life because his life required it. He told himself he would deal with it later. Later did not come.

What came instead, over the decades, was a dull absence that he did not have a name for until much later — a sense that something had been left unfinished, a tendency to become unexpectedly moved in situations that reminded him of his father, a discomfort with Father's Day and the years his children were the age he was when his father died. He did not connect these to grief because the grief had never felt like grief. It had felt like nothing. The nothing was the problem.

At fifty-four, during a period of reduced obligation — the business sold, the children grown — the grief arrived. It came gradually, a belated surfacing of something that had been waiting for room. It surprised him: he had not known how much was still there.

The mirror applied to the past: Did it go well — his relationship with his father, the loss, the way the death was carried? The relationship had its difficulties, as most do, and the good in it went largely unsaid while his father was alive. The death went largely unprocessed for over two decades. No — it did not go well, in the sense that the loss was real and the grief did not have the space it needed when it needed it. Did it truly matter? Yes. This was his father, and the loss shaped James in ways he is only now beginning to trace. Is there anything in his control to change? His father cannot be returned. The unsaid things remain unsaid. The years of deferred grief cannot be un-deferred.

The path is acceptance — of the loss, of the late arrival of the grief, and of the fact that the processing that is happening now, twenty-six years on, is not a failure. It is the grief finding its way through the only opening that was ever available to it. Acceptance here does not mean the grief should stop. It means the fight against having grieved wrong — too late, in the wrong order, without the right rituals — can stop. The grief is real. It arrived when it could. That is enough.

The Future: What Has Not Yet Happened, and How Should I Enter It?

How will this affect the five dimensions? Does this truly matter? How easy is it to reverse if I change my mind?

Future decisions that shape the emotional dimension are usually decisions about relationships and commitments — not about emotions directly. The emotional consequences are significant, and often not obvious in advance. The future question set applied here asks you to see those consequences across the full picture before committing.

[C0611] Caroline is forty-eight and has been considering, for two years, whether to cut contact with her sister. The relationship has been damaging for most of her adult life — her sister is volatile, critical, and consistently leaves Caroline feeling diminished after every interaction. The pattern is not new and has not responded to any of the approaches Caroline has tried: direct conversation, reduced frequency, establishing boundaries, family mediation. After each attempt, the dynamic resets within weeks. The interactions are reliably destabilizing, and Caroline spends days recovering from each one.

She has not cut contact because the sister is her only sibling, because her parents are elderly and the relationship will grow more complicated when they die, and because there is a version of herself she does not want to become — the person who has no relationship with her own family. She also has not maintained contact because it is good for her. She has maintained it because walking away feels like a verdict she is not sure she has the right to deliver.

How will this affect the five dimensions? The emotional gain would be real and immediate: the destabilizing interactions would end, and with them the days-long recovery they require. The disruptions arrive on a reliable cycle; without them, her inner life would have room to stabilize. The connections cost is also real: she would lose the only sibling relationship she has, complicate the family dynamics around her aging parents, and carry whatever it means to be someone who does not speak to her sister. Her identity would be affected — the story she tells about herself and family loyalty would need revision.

Financially and physically, the effects are modest. The picture is not simple.

Does it truly matter? Yes. This is a decision that will shape the texture of her daily life and her sense of herself for years.

How easy is it to reverse? More reversible than it feels from inside the decision. Contact can be restored if circumstances change — if the sister undergoes genuine change, if a family emergency makes it necessary, if Caroline herself decides, years from now, that she wants to try again. Cutting contact is not the same as cutting the possibility of contact. The door can be reopened; opening it again would carry its own cost and complexity, but it is not permanently sealed.

The path is agency — with clear eyes about what it costs and what it recovers. The decision Caroline has been deferring is not whether she has the right to protect her inner life. She does. The decision is whether she has examined the full picture honestly enough to act on it — the gain, the cost, the reversibility — rather than continuing to defer because the decision is hard. The path is agency, entered when the examination is complete.

The emotional dimension is the hardest to see clearly because the instrument of seeing — your capacity for honest self-assessment — is itself affected by what it is trying to examine. A depressed person applying the questions may arrive at answers shaped by the depression. An anxious person may overweight what can go wrong. A person carrying old anger may mistake the feeling for a current threat.

The mirror applied to the emotional dimension asks first where the feeling comes from, and second what to do about it. Getting the source right is what makes the second question answerable. When the picture remains unclear despite honest effort — when the same question produces uncertainty no matter how specifically it is asked — that is a signal the mirror may need to be held by someone else for a while.

VII.

Financial Well-Being

The first two dimensions were internal — your body and your inner life. This dimension deals in numbers. Money is the most measurable dimension of your life. You can count it, track it, compare it, and project it. This concreteness is both the strength of the dimension and the trap it sets, because the clarity of the numbers creates an illusion that the dimension is simple — that more is always better, that the math is all that matters, and that financial problems are always about money. Financial problems are not always about money.

There is a threshold in financial life, and it is different for everyone. Below it, money is functional — you need it to live, to pay bills, to meet the material obligations of your existence. Financial problems below the threshold are concrete and consequential: you cannot make rent, you cannot absorb an unexpected expense, your income does not cover your needs. The questions address them directly.

Above the threshold, something shifts. Your needs are met, and yet the financial goals persist. Money often stops being about money. It becomes about status and identity, about an anxiety that has long since outrun the circumstances that created it. The feelings are genuine, but their source often lies in another dimension. The mirror shows you which side of the threshold you are on and, if you are above it, whether the financial pursuit that consumes your attention is truly financial or whether the real work is elsewhere.

Sufficiency

Sufficiency is the most fundamental financial question: does your income cover your life? Not what you aspire to — your actual life, with its actual expenses, its actual obligations, and its actual needs. Knowing which side of it you stand on is where financial clarity begins.

Most people have an intuitive sense of where they stand, but intuition is unreliable here because financial anxiety distorts perception in both directions. People below the threshold sometimes deny it, telling themselves they are managing when they are accumulating debt. People above the threshold sometimes cannot locate it — carrying a sense of precariousness that has nothing to do with their actual numbers. Look at the math — the objective picture — and let the math inform which question comes next.

[C0701] Robert, forty-seven, earns a steady salary as a facilities manager. His income covers the mortgage, the children, the car, the groceries — the actual life, not the aspirational one. His brother-in-law earns three times as much; his neighbors have newer cars. He describes himself as "getting by," as though adequacy were an apology. Is his financial sufficiency going well? Yes. The path is appreciation. Sufficiency distorted by comparison still looks like sufficiency when the mirror is held honestly.

[C0702] Raymond is thirty-four and does not earn enough. This is not a matter of perception or comparison — it is arithmetic. He works full-time as a warehouse supervisor, and his salary does not cover his family's basic expenses. His wife works part-time around their children's school schedule, and together they fall short by several hundred dollars most months. The gap is filled by credit cards, which are accumulating debt that neither of them talks about openly.

Raymond is not irresponsible. He spends only on necessities. His expenses are housing, food, transportation, childcare, and the modest costs of raising two children in a city where the cost of living has outpaced wages for a decade. He has looked for better-paying work and found that the jobs available to him pay roughly what he earns now. He has considered a second job and calculated that the childcare costs would consume most of the additional income.

Is his financial sufficiency going well? No. His income does not cover his life, and the gap is being filled by debt that is growing. Does it truly matter? Yes — the debt is compounding, the stress is affecting his marriage and his health, and the trajectory, if unchanged, leads somewhere worse. Is it in his control to change? Partially. He can examine expenses for anything reducible, pursue training that might open higher-paying work, seek assistance programs he may not know about. But some of the constraint is structural: the cost of living where he lives, the wages available for his skills, the childcare equation that limits his wife's earning capacity. Raymond cannot will his salary higher or his city cheaper. He can look for the specific points where effort produces results and direct his energy there. The path is agency for what is within reach, and acceptance of the structural constraint that no effort of his can move.

Security

Security is the layer above sufficiency. Sufficiency asks whether you can pay this month's bills. Security asks what happens when something goes wrong — because something, eventually, will. A job loss, a medical emergency, a car that dies, a roof that leaks. Security is the buffer between your life and the shocks that life delivers.

It takes many forms: savings, insurance, transferable skills, a home owned rather than rented. Security is a general condition — the degree to which your financial life can absorb a hit without collapsing — not a single number you can point to.

Like sufficiency, security has a threshold. Below it, the absence of a buffer creates a fragility that colors everything — you cannot take risks, you cannot absorb surprises, and you live with a background awareness that one bad month could unravel years of effort. Above it, the buffer provides a freedom that is easy to undervalue — the freedom to say no to work that is wrong for you, to weather a setback without catastrophe, to make decisions based on what is right rather than what is urgent.

[C0703] Andrea is thirty-nine and has been saving aggressively for fifteen years. She has enough in her accounts to cover several years of expenses. She has no debt and owns her apartment. She maxes out every retirement account available to her.

On paper, this is an unambiguous appreciation case. She has built extraordinary financial security through sustained discipline. She should be the person who recognizes what she has and protects it.

But Andrea cannot stop. She turns down dinners with friends because she calculates the cost. She has not bought new clothes in two years, because spending, regardless of what she can afford, feels dangerous. She earns well, lives far below her means, and feels perpetually on the verge of financial ruin despite every number telling her she is secure.

Andrea grew up in a household where money was a constant source of anxiety. Her parents fought about it. There were stretches where groceries were uncertain. She absorbed the lesson early and completely: money is safety, and you can never have enough of it. She has built a financial fortress, and she lives inside it the way someone who nearly drowned lives around water — with a vigilance that never fully relaxes.

Is her financial security going well? By the numbers, yes — they describe extraordinary security. Her experience of that security is another matter entirely: she does not feel secure, and no amount of savings has changed that. The numbers say appreciation; the experience says something is wrong. Which one do you trust?

You trust the second question. Does it truly matter — does she need more financial security? No. She has enough. More than enough. The problem is not financial at all. It is emotional: the anxiety she carries about money has its source in childhood experience, not in her current numbers. The path is discontinuation of the building — the fortress is already impregnable. The real work is in the emotional dimension, where the childhood anxiety lives and where it might, with attention, begin to loosen.

The Pursuit Beyond Sufficiency

This facet sits above the threshold. When your needs are met and your security is established, the financial questions change. You are no longer asking whether you can pay your bills or survive a shock. You are asking: why am I still pursuing more? What is the additional money for? What number would be enough, and would reaching it actually change how I feel?

These are not financial questions. They are questions about identity, purpose, and self-worth that use money as the vehicle — the thing being accumulated, the score being kept, the metric being tracked. The underlying drive often has its root elsewhere.

The pursuit is most often here to outrun what truly matters, which is why discontinuation appears so frequently in this facet.

[C0704] Glenn is fifty and has built a successful consulting business over twenty years. A few years ago, mid-conversation with his wife, he said something he had never articulated before: "I think we have enough." Not a number — a recognition. The pursuit that had organized his working life had achieved its purpose. The next dollar would not change anything he could name. Is his financial life going well? Yes. He has reached the point where wealth fully supports his life, and he has recognized it — which is the harder part. The path is appreciation.

[C0705] Victor is forty-six and cannot stop. His net worth has crossed into territory that would fund his family's life several times over, and yet he works seventy-hour weeks, tracks his portfolio daily, and experiences genuine anxiety when the numbers dip — even when the dip is meaningless relative to his total position. He has told his wife he will slow down when he reaches a specific number. He reached that number two years ago. The target moved.

Victor is not stupid. He can see, when he is candid with himself, that the pursuit has become its own engine — that the money no longer serves a purpose he can articulate. When pressed, he offers reasons: the children's future, a possible downturn, the desire to leave a legacy. But the children are already provided for, the downturn would have to be unprecedented to threaten his position, and the legacy he is building at the cost of seventy-hour weeks is one his children would trade for more of his time.

Is his financial pursuit going well? By the numbers, yes. By the life, no — the hours, the anxiety, the distance from his family, the inability to stop. Does it truly matter? This is the question Victor has never asked candidly. The additional money he is pursuing serves no function he can name. It does not improve his sufficiency, which was achieved long ago. It does not improve his security, which is already extensive. The pursuit grips him — but when the mirror asks why, the answer leads away from the financial dimension entirely. It leads to identity: Victor's sense of self is built on achievement and accumulation, and without the pursuit, he does not know who he is.

The path is discontinuation of the financial goal — the next million will not change his life — combined with the recognition that the energy he recovers from the pursuit needs somewhere to go. That somewhere is the identity dimension, where the question he has never had to sit with is waiting: who is he without the number — the thing that has organized his days, justified the hours, and given him a self-concept that is always in the process of being earned? The path into that question is agency in the identity dimension.

Financial Behavior and Habits

Beneath the numbers are patterns — the habits that shape how you interact with money daily. Avoidance is common: never looking at the accounts, never opening the statements, keeping the picture deliberately blurry. So is its opposite — impulsive spending driven by feeling rather than need. And then there is hoarding: holding money so tightly that the security it provides is canceled out by the anxiety the holding produces. These patterns are often invisible to the person living them, driven by emotional associations with money formed long before the person had any money of their own. The questions apply: is the behavior going well, does it truly matter, and is it in your control to change? For most behavioral patterns, the answer to the third question is yes — these are learned habits, and learned habits can be unlearned.

Other Facets

Other facets of financial well-being include generational wealth and poverty, financial dependence on a partner, the cost of caregiving, retirement anxiety, and the intersection of financial well-being with health care costs. Each can be examined with the same questions.

The Past: What Happened in This Dimension, and How Should I Carry It?

Did it go well? Did it truly matter? Is there anything still in my control to change?

The financial past is unlike the emotional past in one important way: its consequences are concrete and present. A financial decision made in your thirties may still be shaping your position in your fifties in ways that can be calculated, not just felt. What you carry from this dimension's past is often not a feeling about what happened but the actual changed position that resulted from it — the retirement account that was never rebuilt, the debt that was eventually paid but at a cost that compounded for years.

The past question set in the financial dimension asks not only whether you have made peace with what happened but whether there is any agency that remains — any course still open that deserves your attention.

[C0706] Patrick is fifty-four. In his mid-thirties he invested most of his savings in a startup founded by a close friend. The business model was credible and the friend was trustworthy. The due diligence Patrick did was reasonable for someone without professional investment experience. The company failed four years later, and Patrick lost everything he had put in — which was, at the time, nearly a decade of careful saving.

He did not recover financially for years. His retirement savings, which should have been compounding through his thirties and forties, were rebuilt from scratch at forty, then again at forty-four after a divorce that divided what he had managed to accumulate. He is now in a position that is stable and sufficient — he earns well, his expenses are under control, and he is saving seriously again. But he will retire with significantly less than he would have had the investment not failed, and that gap, which he can calculate with reasonable precision, is not going to close.

The mirror applied to the past: Did it go well? No. The investment failed and the financial consequence was large and lasting. Did it truly matter? Yes — the gap in his retirement position is real and present. Is there anything in his control to change? The investment cannot be undone. The years of compounding he lost cannot be recovered. What remains open is the present and the future: the savings rate he maintains now, the decisions he makes about risk and asset allocation going forward, the choices still available about when to retire and how to structure the years that remain. These are genuine forms of agency, and they matter even if they cannot fully close the gap.

The path is acceptance for what happened and agency for what remains open. Patrick has spent time, in the years since the loss, running the counterfactual — imagining the retirement account as it would be, calculating the compounding he missed. The counterfactual is accurate. It is also, at this point, consuming energy that belongs to the future rather than the past. Acceptance here is not an endorsement of the investment. It means that the calculation of what was lost has been completed, the lesson has been absorbed, and continued rehearsal of the counterfactual is no longer producing anything except the rehearsal itself. The path is acceptance of what happened and agency directed at what comes next.

[C0707] Judith is fifty-one and checks her bank balance every morning. She has done this for as long as she can remember — a reflex as automatic as brushing her teeth, and far from as neutral. The morning balance check is accompanied by a low-grade anxiety that persists through the first hours of the day, a scan for what might go wrong, a mental calculation of upcoming expenses against current funds.

Her balance is always fine. It has been fine for over fifteen years. Judith is a senior administrator at a university, earns a salary that comfortably exceeds her expenses, has a pension she has been contributing to for two decades, and maintains a savings cushion her financial advisor describes as conservative but solid. There is no morning on which the balance presents a genuine problem. The anxiety does not know this.

She grew up in a family where money was genuinely precarious — a father who worked seasonally, a mother who managed the household on an income that fluctuated with the weather and the economy. There were winters when the heat was rationed. There were Christmases when the presents were fewer than the children knew to want. Judith was the oldest child and understood the family's financial situation earlier than her siblings. She learned to track the numbers because the numbers, when she was a child, actually mattered — a shift in them signaled a real change in what the family could do, eat, or count on.

The mirror applied to the past: Did the vigilance go well — was the childhood monitoring of the family's finances appropriate to the situation? Yes. Watching the numbers closely, in a household where the numbers were genuinely fragile, was not anxiety — it was appropriate attention to real circumstances. Did it truly matter? Yes — the family's financial situation during her childhood was real, and the vigilance Judith developed in response to it was a reasonable adaptation.

Is there anything in her control to change? The childhood cannot be revised. But the vigilance she developed in response to it is present, not past — she is practicing it every morning. And the question the past question set opens: did the vigilance that served her then still serve her now? The circumstances that warranted it have resolved. The numbers she is watching are not fragile. The morning check is a habit formed in a different financial reality, maintained into a current one where it no longer has useful work to do.

The path is discontinuation — not of financial attention, which is appropriate, but of the anxiety-driven vigilance that was calibrated for a childhood scarcity that no longer exists. This is distinct from Andrea's case, where the anxiety operates in the present and its emotional source still needs to be examined. Judith has already identified the source — she knows exactly where the morning check comes from. What she has not yet done is decide that the past that generated it is finished, and that a reflex formed in one financial reality does not have to govern a different one. The path is discontinuation of the reflex, not of the awareness it distorts.

The Future: What Has Not Yet Happened, and How Should I Enter It?

How will this affect the five dimensions? Does this truly matter? How easy is it to reverse if I change my mind?

Financial futures are among the most concrete decisions the mirror encounters — the numbers can often be projected, the tradeoffs calculated, the reversibility estimated with some precision. What the future question set adds is structure: it prevents the financial analysis from running in isolation and puts reversibility in view before the commitment is made.

[C0708] Lydia is forty-three and has spent seventeen years as a corporate attorney. She is good at it, well compensated, and increasingly certain that she does not want to do it for another twenty years. What she wants — has wanted, quietly, for several years — is to teach. High school history. She has a genuine passion for the subject and a growing conviction that the work she wants to do with the time she has left is not the work she is currently doing.

The financial picture is the obstacle, or feels like one. Her current salary is substantial. A starting teacher's salary, in the district where she lives, is roughly a third of what she earns now. She has a mortgage, two children approaching college age, and a lifestyle built around an income she would be abandoning.

How will this affect the five dimensions? Financially, the cut would be significant and immediate — her monthly income would fall sharply, the college funding plan would require revision, and some of the discretionary spending that structures her current life would need to stop. The transition would likely take two years, including certification requirements, and during that period her income would be lower than it has been at any point in her adult life. Emotionally, she has been carrying a low-grade dissatisfaction with her current work for years; removing it would be significant. Physically, the demands of corporate law — the hours, the sustained pressure — would give way to something different in texture if not lighter in effort. Her connections would shift — some professional relationships would fade, new ones would form. Her identity would change substantially: she would stop being who she has been professionally for nearly two decades.

Does it truly matter? When she examines this honestly: yes. The income gap is real but survivable. The deeper question is what she wants her working life to be for. She has been successful at a thing she does not love, and the alternative she is considering is something she believes she would love.

How easy is it to reverse? More reversible than it feels from inside the anxiety. Law licenses do not expire, and attorneys return to practice after career breaks. The path back is not seamless — she would likely need to reenter at a lower level and rebuild — but it exists. She is not choosing irrevocably. She is choosing with a reversibility window she understands.

The path is agency — entered with clear eyes about the financial adjustment required and with the reversibility window explicitly in view. The question the mirror has been turning for her is not whether the pay cut is large. It is whether the gap between what she earns and what she needs is bridgeable, and whether a bridgeable gap is a sufficient reason to continue doing work that no longer suits who she is. It is not. The path is agency.

[C0709] Edward is fifty-eight and has been offered the opportunity to sell his stake in the manufacturing business he cofounded thirty years ago. The offer is serious — a credible buyer, at a valuation beyond anything he imagined when he started the company. He has until the end of the quarter to decide.

The money, if he takes it, would be transformative — enough to fund the rest of his life at any reasonable level of spending, with significant inheritance left over. He would no longer need to work. He could do whatever comes next from a position of complete financial independence.

He is not sure he wants to sell. Not because the number is wrong — the number is right, perhaps better than right. He is not sure because the business is the organizing structure of his adult life, and he does not know what replaces it. He has not built a picture of what comes after, and the absence of that picture makes the decision feel like standing at an edge rather than stepping through a door.

How will this affect the five dimensions? Financially, the transformation is complete — he would move from significant but illiquid wealth tied to the business to liquid, diversified financial independence. Emotionally, the business has been the container of his identity, his daily purpose, and much of his social world for three decades; removing it will produce something significant, and he cannot yet name what. His connections would change — his relationship with the cofounders, with the employees he has known for years, with the customers and vendors who are part of his daily life — all of these would shift. Physically, the demands of running the business would end; he would gain time and lose structure. His identity would require rebuilding in ways that are not yet clear.

Does it truly matter? Yes — this is a decision that will define the shape of the decades that remain.

How easy is it to reverse? It is not reversible. Once the stake is sold, the business continues without him. He cannot buy back in on the same terms, and the role he currently occupies —

founder, coowner, daily participant — will not exist after the sale. The real question is not what happens to the business. It is what happens to him.

This is the case where the third question governs. The offer may be exactly right — the valuation, the timing, the buyer. But the irreversibility of the decision means the certainty required before committing is higher than for a choice that could be unwound. Edward's hesitation is not irrational. It may be the appropriate weight being given to a permanent change by someone who has not yet finished the examination the decision requires. What does he want the next chapter to look like? Who is he when he is not running the business? Has he built any picture of what comes after, or has he been avoiding the question because the business has always provided the answer?

If those questions remain unexamined, the commitment is premature. The path — for now — is completing the examination, so that when he commits, he commits with the clarity that an irreversible decision demands. The path, for now, is agency — not the agency of signing the documents, but the agency of completing the examination the decision requires: building a picture of what comes after, answering the identity questions he has been avoiding, and arriving at the certainty that an irreversible sale deserves before it is made.

Above the threshold, money often stops being about money. It becomes about status, identity, and the need to be seen in particular ways. That is the financial dimension revealing the edge of the next one. Connections adds something none of the first three dimensions contained: another person's will. You can change your habits, redirect your feelings, restructure your finances. You cannot change another person. The mirror, applied to your relationships, will show you what you bring and what you cannot control — and the line between them is where the hardest work lives.

VIII.

Connections

The first three dimensions belonged to you alone. This one belongs to the space between you and other people, and that space is not entirely in your hands.

You do not live alone. The people around you affect your mood, your health, your decisions, your sense of who you are, and your capacity for everything else. A single good relationship can sustain a person through extraordinary difficulty. A single bad one can undermine a life that looks, from every other angle, whole. This dimension includes the relationships that nourish and the ones that drain.

You can control what you bring to a relationship, how you respond within it, and — crucially — whether you remain in it. You cannot control what someone else does, feels, or decides. Agency in a relationship is always partial.

Intimate Partnership

An intimate partnership — marriage, a long-term relationship, or whatever form it takes — is, for most people, the single most consequential relationship in their life. It is the relationship that shares your home, your children, your finances, your daily rhythms, and your decisions about the future. When it works, it is a foundation as solid as physical health or financial security. When it falters, its effects reach into every other dimension.

This facet also includes the absence of a partnership — the state of being single, whether by choice, by circumstance, or by loss. The questions apply to the absence just as they apply to the presence, and the answer may be any of the four paths.

[C0801] Janet is fifty-three and Keith is fifty-four, and they have been married for twenty-two years. Neither of them would describe it as exciting. What they would struggle to describe — because it has become invisible through familiarity — is how thoroughly it works: the responsibilities divided without negotiation, the disagreements that do not escalate, the room they give each other, the difficult years they came through without the relationship breaking. Is their intimate partnership going well? Yes. Not perfectly, not excitingly, but functionally and deeply — built through two decades of small, unglamorous decisions that neither of them had to think about because they made them together. The path is appreciation.

[C0802] Renee is thirty-seven and knows her marriage is in trouble. She has known for over a year. The arguments have increased — not about big things, but about everything, which is worse. The tone between her and her husband has shifted from warmth to wariness. They are polite in front of the children and distant when they are alone. She has begun dreading evenings, which used to be the part of the day she looked forward to most.

When Renee examines what changed, she finds that it did not happen suddenly. It accumulated. She took on more responsibility at work and brought the stress home. Her husband started a business that consumes his weekends and most of his emotional bandwidth. They stopped having the small conversations that used to knit their days together — the check-ins, the debriefs, the casual intimacy of two people who are paying attention to each other. They did not decide to drift. They drifted because neither of them was watching.

Is her intimate partnership going well? No. The connection has deteriorated, and the deterioration is accelerating. Does it truly matter? Yes — this is the central relationship in her life, it is affecting her happiness, her children's environment, and her sense of the future. Is it in her control to change? Partially. Renee cannot fix the marriage alone — it involves another person, and her husband's willingness to engage is not something she controls. But she can initiate the conversation she has been avoiding and name what she sees. She can suggest they get help. She can change what she brings to the relationship, even if she cannot guarantee what he brings. The path is agency — partial, uncertain, dependent on another person's response, but real. The alternative — continuing to drift in silence — is avoidance, and avoidance in a relationship erodes it.

[C0803] Gloria is fifty-nine and has been married for thirty-one years to a man she loves and who will not change.

She would not have said it that way five years ago. Five years ago she would have said he was working on it, that they were making progress, that the latest approach — a new therapist, a book she had found, a conversation she had planned — was going to be the one that finally reached him. She would have said this with conviction, because she had said it dozens of times before, and each time she believed it.

Her husband is emotionally reserved. He has always been emotionally reserved. He withholds affection, guards his feelings, and avoids the kind of emotional intimacy that Gloria craves and has craved for the duration of their marriage. He is a good man — faithful, responsible, present, devoted to their children. He is also, in the dimension that matters most to Gloria, unavailable.

She has tried every approach available to her. Direct requests. Letters. Books left on his nightstand. Couples therapy, which he attended dutifully and from which he absorbed nothing that changed his daily behavior. She has asked, pleaded, explained, and demonstrated. He has tried, briefly and sincerely, and returned each time to his default.

Here is where the mess lives: Gloria knows this. She has known it for years. And she has continued to try anyway, because stopping felt like a betrayal — of the marriage, of him, of the version of herself that refuses to give up on the people she loves. She has told herself that persistence is virtue, that good wives keep trying, that the next conversation might be different. She keeps hoping, and the hoping keeps her from seeing what thirty-one years of evidence has already shown. Underneath the hope, there is anger — anger at him for being who he is, anger at herself for needing what she needs, anger at the situation for being unsolvable. She does not express the anger because it contradicts the narrative she has built: that she is patient, that she is understanding, that she is still working on it.

The questions cut through this. Is her intimate partnership going well? In some ways, yes — the partnership is stable, the practical foundation is solid, and the commitment is genuine. In the facet of emotional intimacy, no — Gloria's need is unmet and has been unmet for the duration of the marriage. Does it truly matter? Yes. This is not a trivial preference. Emotional intimacy is central to how Gloria experiences a relationship, and its absence is a real and sustained source of pain. Is it in her control to change? She has tried, extensively and sincerely. Her husband has tried too, within his capacity. The gap between what she needs and what he can provide appears to be permanent — he is unable, in a way that thirty-one years of evidence has confirmed, to give her what she most needs.

The path is acceptance. Not acceptance of a loveless marriage — the marriage contains love, expressed differently than she would choose. But acceptance that this specific need will not be met within this relationship, and that the energy she has spent trying to change something that will not change — the hope, the strategies, the anger she will not name — can be redirected. Toward a realistic picture of what this partnership is rather than what she wishes it were. Acceptance asks Gloria to stop waiting for a different result, and to start building a life that is honest about the result she already has.

Family

Family is the set of relationships you did not choose but that shaped you more than almost anything else. Your parents, your siblings, your children — these are bonds defined not by preference but by blood, by proximity, by the shared history of having grown up in the same house or having raised someone together. They carry a weight that chosen relationships rarely match, because you often cannot leave them, even when the relationship is doing you harm.

Family relationships are also where expectations are highest and where the gap between expectation and reality produces the most pain. You expect your parents to love you well. You expect your siblings to be loyal. You expect your children to thrive. When these expectations are met, the result is a form of well-being so fundamental it is almost invisible. When they are not, the pain is as deep as the well-being is invisible.

[C0804] Sylvia is thirty-eight and has spent most of her adult life managing her relationship with her mother. Managing is the right word — not enjoying, not deepening, but managing, the way you might manage a chronic condition that requires constant attention and produces no cure.

Her mother is critical, anxious, and intrusive. She comments on Sylvia's weight, her parenting, her husband, her career — not occasionally but reliably, every visit, every call. She does this not out of malice but out of a genuine inability to separate her own anxiety from her daughter's life. She loves Sylvia. She also makes Sylvia feel, after every interaction, like she is failing at something.

Sylvia has tried to address this. She has set boundaries, which her mother respects for a few weeks and then forgets. She has had direct conversations, which her mother agrees with in the moment and does not change afterward. She has reduced contact, which produces guilt that is almost worse than the criticism. She has tried therapy, which helped her understand the dynamic but did not change her mother.

Is her family relationship with her mother going well? No. The relationship is a reliable source of stress and self-doubt. Does it truly matter? Yes — it is her mother, and the relationship affects her mood, her self-image, and her ability to be present in the rest of her life. Is it in her control to change? She has tried, extensively. Her mother is not going to become a different person. The criticism is not going to stop, and the anxiety that drives it will not resolve. What Sylvia can control is how she carries the relationship — the frequency of contact, the boundaries she maintains even when they are not respected, the internal narrative she tells herself after each interaction. The path is acceptance of her mother as she is and ongoing agency over her own responses. Acceptance does not mean absorbing the criticism. It means stopping the expectation that her mother will change, and building a relationship that is sustainable given who her mother actually is rather than who Sylvia wishes she were.

[C0805] Helen is fifty-five, and her brother is the person she calls when she does not know what to do. He is three years older, lives two hours away, and they talk most Sundays — not about anything in particular, not with an agenda, just the ongoing conversation of two people who have known each other longer than they have known anyone else. He remembers things about her childhood that she has forgotten. She remembers things about his. Between them, they hold a version of the past that neither could hold alone.

The relationship is not effortless — it survived a period in their thirties when they barely spoke, a disagreement about their mother's care that turned bitter before it turned honest, and a stretch of years when their lives were so different that the connection felt more like obligation than choice. What brought them back was a series of small decisions rather than any dramatic reconciliation: he called after her surgery, she drove up when his wife left, they kept showing up when it would have been easier to let the distance settle into permanence.

Is her family relationship with her brother going well? Yes — and the yes carries a weight that surprises her when she pauses to feel it. This is not the obligatory closeness of people who share parents and holidays. It is the earned closeness of two people who almost lost each other and chose not to. When Helen thinks about what she would miss if the Sunday calls stopped — the feeling of being known by someone who has seen every version of her, which no exchanged information could replace — it is a warmth she does not usually pause long enough to notice. The path is appreciation. The relationship is good, it was not always good, and the distance between those two facts is the measure of what they built.

[C0806] Paul is forty-eight and nearly lost his daughter. Not to illness or accident — to distance. His daughter is twenty-four, and in the years after she left for college, their relationship deteriorated steadily. The calls became shorter, then less frequent, then obligatory. When she came home for holidays, the visits were polite and hollow — two people performing a relationship that had stopped functioning underneath the performance.

Paul knew what had gone wrong, or at least he knew the shape of it. He had been a rigid father — controlling about grades, critical about her choices, dismissive of interests he did not understand. He had parented the way his father had parented him: with standards, with judgment, with the assumption that love was expressed through correction rather than acceptance. His daughter had absorbed it the way children do — silently, completely — and left as soon as she could.

The realization that he was losing her arrived slowly and then all at once. A birthday call she did not return. A holiday she spent with a friend's family instead of his. A text message so brief it could have been sent to a stranger. He sat with the accumulation of these moments and understood, with a clarity that was physically painful, that his daughter was not punishing him. She was protecting herself. And the distance was a reasonable response to how he had treated her.

Is his family relationship with his daughter going well? No — the relationship has eroded to near-absence, and he traces the erosion to his behavior. Does it truly matter? Yes — more than his pride, more than his discomfort, more than the story he told himself about being a good father who held high standards. Is it in his control to change? This is the question that haunts him the most. He cannot undo the years of rigidity. He cannot make her trust him by deciding she should. But he can change what he brings to the relationship from this point forward. He can apologize — not the defensive kind that explains the intention behind the behavior, but the kind that names the behavior and its effect without qualification. He can stop correcting. He can ask about her life and listen to the answer without steering it. He can become, slowly and without guarantee that it will work, a different kind of father — not the one he was wired to be, but the one she needed.

Paul made the call. The first conversation was stiff. The second was slightly less so. Six months later, the calls are not what they were before college — they may never be — but they are real. She told him about a problem at work last month without him offering a solution, and the restraint nearly killed him, and it was the most important thing he has done as a parent in years. The path is agency — slow and humbling, the kind that requires a person to change the thing about themselves that is causing the damage.

Friendships and Community

Friendships are the relationships you choose — and because you choose them, they reveal something about you that family and partnership do not. The people you spend time with by preference, not obligation, say something about what you value, what you enjoy, and who you are when you are not playing a role assigned by blood or commitment.

Friendships also have a feature that makes them both more flexible and more fragile than family: they can end without drama, simply by fading. A friendship that was once central can become peripheral, then absent, without either person making a conscious decision to let it go. This is not always a loss. Sometimes it is the natural conclusion of a connection that served a period of your life and has run its course. Sometimes it is a loss — a good thing that was neglected until it disappeared.

Community is the broader layer: the neighborhoods, the groups, the organizations, the social fabric that gives you a sense of belonging or leaves you without one. It is harder to examine than individual friendships because it is diffuse, but its presence or absence affects your life profoundly.

[C0807] Charlotte is thirty-four and is lonely. Not the dramatic loneliness of complete isolation — she has colleagues, acquaintances, a sister she is close to, and a boyfriend she has been seeing for several months. But she lacks the layer of friendship that she sees in other people's lives and that she remembers having in her own: the people you call for no reason, the people who know your daily life in detail, the people who would notice if you disappeared for a week.

Charlotte lost this layer gradually. She moved cities for work at twenty-eight and left behind the social world she had built through college and her twenties. She intended to rebuild it. Six years later, she has not, and the gap has become harder to close with each passing year. Making friends as an adult is different from making friends in college — there is no shared dormitory, no built-in proximity, no natural occasion to spend unstructured time with new people. The friendships Charlotte has attempted have been pleasant but have not deepened, stalling at the level of occasional plans that both parties cancel as often as they keep.

Is her social life going well? No. She is lonely in a specific and identifiable way — she lacks close friendships, and the lack affects her emotional well-being and her sense of belonging. Does it truly matter? Yes. Charlotte feels it — the absence every weekend, every evening, every time something happens that she wants to share with someone who is not there. Is it in her control to change? Yes, though the effort required is substantial and the timeline is uncertain. Friendships form slowly — they require proximity, repeated contact, vulnerability, and time. But Charlotte can create the conditions: joining groups aligned with her interests, showing up consistently, initiating plans rather than waiting to be invited, tolerating the awkwardness of early-stage adult friendship. The path is agency — sustained, patient, and unglamorous. Building a social life from scratch is among the harder forms of agency this dimension contains, but it is within her control, and the alternative — waiting for friendships to arrive — is not a strategy.

[C0808] Walter is sixty-one and has four friends. He does not use the word loosely. He means four people, outside his family, who he trusts completely, who know the parts of his life he does not advertise, and who would come if he called at two in the morning. He has had these friendships for between fifteen and thirty years. They are not effortless — they are maintained through consistent, unglamorous investment: the standing monthly dinner, the calls that happen whether or not there is news, the willingness to show up for the difficult things and not only the easy ones.

He is aware that this is unusual. Many of the men he knows his age have let their friendships thin to the point of disappearance — consumed by work in their thirties, by family in their forties, by a habit of self-sufficiency that hardens into isolation by their fifties. Walter did not escape this by accident. He escaped it because his closest friend had a heart attack at forty-three, and the weeks Walter spent at the hospital — the person the family called when they needed someone there overnight, present in a way that mere visitors are not — showed him what the friendship was actually worth. He decided, consciously and specifically, that he would not let the rest of them fade.

Is his social life going well? Yes. The four friendships are among the most valuable things in his life, and he knows it — not in the way you know a fact, but in the way you know something you almost lost. The path is appreciation, and Walter's case makes visible what appreciation means when it is not passive. He does not simply notice the friendships are good. He maintains them with the deliberate attention other people reserve for their health or their finances. The friendships are good because he decided they would be, and he keeps deciding.

Loneliness and Isolation

Loneliness is the gap between the connections you have and the connections you need. It is the arithmetic of a long life when the circle shrinks — when the people who knew you when you were young leave one by one, and the kind of friendship built over fifty years cannot be built over five. The new city where you know no one. The crowded room where you feel invisible. Loneliness is not the same as being alone — some people are alone and not lonely, and some people are surrounded by others and profoundly lonely. The gap is subjective, which makes it harder to assess from the outside, but it is real, and its effects are as measurable as any physical condition.

Loneliness can be situational — the result of a move, a life transition, a loss — or it can be chronic, a persistent state regardless of the social opportunities available. The mirror helps distinguish between them: situational loneliness often has clear agency — change the circumstances, seek new connections, invest in existing ones. Chronic loneliness is different. When the questions applied in the connections dimension do not resolve it, the source may live elsewhere. Trace the loneliness before deciding where the work needs to happen.

[C0809] Owen is fifty-eight and has been lonely for most of his adult life. He can say this now, though it has taken years to say it without shame. He has been married for twenty-six years to a woman he loves. He has three adult children he is close to. He has colleagues he likes and neighbors who wave. He is not isolated in any observable sense. He is profoundly lonely in a way that none of these connections has ever been able to touch.

The loneliness runs deeper than the number of people in his life. It has been present since adolescence, in some form, through every configuration of his social world. In college, surrounded by people his age. In his twenties, when friendships were easy to form. In his marriage, lying beside a woman who loves him, feeling a distance he cannot explain and has never been able to close. He has made friends, lost them, made more. He has invested in his marriage. He has been present for his children. The loneliness does not respond to any of this. It is there before the effort and after it, unchanged.

The questions, applied to the connections dimension: Is his social life going well? He has connections. The loneliness persists. The first question, applied at the dimension level, does not resolve — which is the signal. The source is not in connections. Does it truly matter? Yes — it is one of the defining facts of his interior life, present in every decade, shaping how he experiences everything else. Is it in his control to change? He has tried, extensively, in the connections dimension. The question of control shifts when the source is traced. For Owen, the loneliness lives in the identity and emotional dimensions — in a difficulty making contact with his own interior life that makes genuine contact with other people's interior lives nearly impossible. The aloneness he feels around others is the aloneness he feels within himself. This is a problem that lives elsewhere — more connections alone cannot solve. The work — learning to be present to his own experience, understanding why the interior self remains at a distance — is where the agency actually lives. The path is agency, directed not at the connections dimension, which is not the source, but at the identity and emotional dimensions where the real work needs to happen.

Professional Relationships

You spend more of your waking hours with colleagues than with almost anyone else. A supportive manager can make a demanding job sustainable. A difficult colleague can make an easy job unbearable. Professional relationships deserve examination through the questions, though they rarely arrive presorted. The question of whether a workplace relationship is going well often turns out, on examination, to be a question about another dimension — financial (is the job still worth what it costs?), identity (is this work still mine?), emotional (is the difficulty the relationship or the state I bring to it?). The first question to ask is not whether the relationship is going well, but where the difficulty actually lives.

[C0810] Adriana is forty-three and has worked for the same manager for four years. In the first two, the relationship was the best she had experienced at work: he advocated for her, gave her latitude, and was genuinely interested in her development. In the past eighteen months something shifted. The latitude contracted. His feedback became critical in ways that feel personal rather than professional. She has been passed over for two assignments she expected to get. She spends Sunday evenings dreading the week, and the dread is specifically about him.

Is her professional relationship going well? No — there is a clear deterioration with a specific person in a specific role. Does it truly matter? Yes — her manager controls her assignments, her advancement, and much of her daily experience of the job. Is it in her control to change? Partially, and the partial is where the real examination begins. She can have a direct conversation with him about what she is observing — the assignments, the feedback, what she might be missing. She can determine whether the shift reflects something about her performance, something about his situation, or something structural that is not about her at all. And if none of these produce a change that makes the relationship workable, she can examine whether the job itself still deserves what she is paying to stay in it. The path is agency — the direct agency of naming what she is experiencing and finding out whether anything can be done about it, before concluding that leaving is the only answer.

Compassion

Compassion — the capacity to see another person's suffering and respond to it with care — is a quality of presence, not a technique or a practice. It is a quality of attention. Like every facet of connections, it can go well or badly, and it can be examined with the same questions.

Compassion can be full and sustaining — the person who moves through the world with a genuine regard for others, who notices when someone is struggling and responds with presence rather than advice. It can be depleted — the nurse, the teacher, the caregiver who gave until there was nothing left and now feels nothing where the compassion used to be. And it can be selective in ways worth examining — generous toward strangers and absent toward the people closest to you, or present for everyone except yourself. Is your capacity for compassion going well? If it has been depleted, does restoring it truly matter? And if it does, is restoration within your reach — through rest, through boundaries, through the recognition that compassion for others that destroys you is not sustainable and is not, in the end, compassion at all?

[C0811] Denise is forty-seven and has worked as a palliative care nurse for sixteen years. For most of that time, she was what the profession calls a natural: she could be fully present with a dying patient and their family, absorb the weight of what was happening, and leave work without carrying it home in a way that broke her. She understood, without being able to explain it, how to be in the room without being destroyed by the room.

Three years ago that capacity began to erode. She cannot point to a single patient or event that broke it. It accumulated, the way fatigue accumulates — not in any single shift but in the compound weight of shift after shift without adequate recovery. Now when she enters a patient's room she feels a distance she does not want to feel, a careful numbness that protects her and that she recognizes as not being fully present. She is still competent. She is no longer, in the way she was, there.

Is her compassion going well? No — it has been depleted, and the depletion is visible to her even if not yet to her patients. Does it truly matter? Yes — it matters to the quality of care she provides, to her sense of herself as a nurse, and to the cost of continuing work she can no longer do in the way it deserves to be done. Is it in her control to change? The depletion has a source: sixteen years without adequate rest, without the supervision and processing that her early career provided, without the recognition that even natural capacity has limits. The path is agency — not toward leaving the work she loves, but toward the conditions that might restore what the work has consumed. More deliberate recovery between difficult periods. Clinical supervision. The boundaries she has been forgoing because the unit is understaffed and she has always been the one who stays. Compassion that is not replenished runs out. Denise knows this. The path is agency: act on the knowledge before the depletion becomes permanent.

Other Facets

Other facets of connections include physical and sexual intimacy within partnerships — a facet shaped by both bodies and emotions, where mismatched desire, changing function, or unspoken needs can erode a relationship that is otherwise strong. Also included are relationships with ex-partners, the challenges of long-distance relationships, the evolving nature of relationships with aging parents, online connections, the caregiver relationship, and the broader sense of community and belonging. Each can be examined with the same questions.

The Past: What Happened in This Dimension, and How Should I Carry It?

Did it go well? Did it truly matter? Is there anything still in my control to change?

The connections past is unlike the financial past: what you carry here is a presence that is simply absent — a friendship that ended, a relationship that broke, a person who is gone. You cannot calculate it the way you calculate a changed financial position. What the past question set asks in this dimension is whether the loss has been honestly examined — whether the third question has been asked in full, including the possibility that something still open has been left untried.

The most important distinction is between losses where agency remains and losses where it does not. The difference is not always obvious from inside the grief, but the mirror can help locate it.

[C0812] Ian is forty-nine and has not spoken to his closest friend from his twenties in fourteen years. The falling-out was real: a conflict over money during a period when both men were under financial pressure, accusations made in anger, a failure to repair in the weeks after when repair would still have been easy. Each of them waited for the other to reach out. Neither did. A few months became a year, and then years, and then the silence became its own fact — something that had gone on too long to breach without the breach being its own event.

Ian thinks about Wesley — his oldest friend — more than he tells anyone. He thinks about him at the kinds of moments Wesley would have understood: a difficulty at work that Wesley would have navigated in a way he'd recognize, a baseball game that reminds him of the season they followed together, the birth of his second child, where Wesley was supposed to be. The loss is not abstract. It is specific and recurring, arriving in the same moments over and over.

He has not reached out because the longer it goes, the stranger it feels. What do you say after fourteen years? He has told himself the friendship is probably not what it was, that Wesley has moved on, that the attempt might produce rejection or awkwardness that would be worse than the silence. He has run the scenarios to convince himself that reaching out would likely fail.

The mirror applied to the past: Did the friendship go well? For most of its duration, yes — it was one of the central friendships of his adult life. Did it truly matter? Yes. A friendship that resurfaces in specific recurring moments for fourteen years is not one he has moved past. Is there anything in his control to change?

This is the question he has not answered honestly. He has told himself the answer is no — that the window closed, that too much time has passed, that Wesley has probably not thought about it the way he has. But he does not actually know this. He has not asked. The conclusion he has reached — that repair would fail — is a conclusion drawn without evidence, from inside the discomfort of a risk he has never taken. The outcome of reaching out is genuinely unknown because reaching out has never been tried.

The path is agency. Not because repair is guaranteed — it is not. Wesley may not respond. The friendship may not be what it was. The attempt may be uncomfortable and produce nothing. But Ian has been treating an untested possibility as a confirmed outcome, and the difference matters. He is carrying the loss of a friendship that may not be as lost as he has decided it is. The path is agency: one attempt, honestly made, which is the only thing that can answer the question he has been living inside for fourteen years.

[C0813] Miriam is sixty-three and her sister Bridget died four years ago, eight months after a diagnosis neither of them expected. The death was not sudden — there was time, and they used some of it. But there were things Miriam did not say, because she assumed there was more time than there was, because some of what needed saying was difficult, and because the habit of their relationship was to communicate around the hard things rather than through them.

Bridget died on a Tuesday afternoon in November. The last real conversation — not the bedside ones, which were constrained by tubes and exhaustion, but a conversation in which both of them were fully present — was three weeks before the end. In that conversation, Miriam did not say what she most needed to say. She told herself she would say it at the next visit. There were two more visits. She did not say it.

She has been sitting with this for four years. Not as a wound she cannot stop reopening — more as a weight she has learned to carry without quite accepting that she will carry it always. She still catches herself composing what she would have said. She still considers it unfinished.

The mirror applied to the past: Did it go well — her relationship with her sister, the time they had, the way the end was navigated? The relationship itself was good — complicated and close in the way of sisters who have shared a long history and who were, in spite of everything, one of each other's primary people. The end did not go well — there was something she needed to say and did not, and the omission has weighed on her since. Did it truly matter? Yes. The unsaid thing was real, and its remaining unsaid left something unfinished that she has been trying to complete in her mind ever since. Is there anything in her control to change? Bridget cannot be returned. The conversation cannot be had. There is no version of agency that reaches her sister now.

The path is acceptance — of the loss, and of the specific loss within the loss: the conversation that did not happen and cannot now happen. Not acceptance as a destination she will one day arrive at, but as the ongoing practice of releasing the fight against a fact that will not change. This is the hardest form of acceptance the connections dimension contains — not accepting a person as they are, but accepting the permanent closure of a door that was left ajar. Miriam may always carry what she did not say. Acceptance is not putting it down. It is stopping the fight against a permanent fact.

The Future: What Has Not Yet Happened, and How Should I Enter It?

How will this affect the five dimensions? Does this truly matter? How easy is it to reverse if I change my mind?

Relational futures are different from financial or physical futures in one important way: they almost always involve another person whose response you cannot predict or control. The future question set applied to the connections dimension helps you see the full picture of what a relational commitment will cost and return — across all five dimensions — before entering it, and to understand the reversibility with honesty rather than optimism.

[C0814] Priya is thirty-six and is deciding whether to have a child. She and her husband have been discussing it, circling it, and partially deciding it for three years. They are in agreement — both want a child — but have not moved from agreement to action. She is the one who has most directly felt the pause as a decision that cannot be indefinitely deferred.

She knows she wants to be a parent. She is uncertain about what it will cost. She has watched her closest friends navigate the first years of parenthood with a mix of wonder and exhaustion that she has found hard to interpret. She works in a demanding field and has spent a decade building a career that she loves. Her marriage is strong but has not been tested at this scale. She is, for the first time, genuinely asking the question rather than circling it.

How will this affect the five dimensions? Financially, she and her husband have examined the numbers and the picture is manageable — demanding but not prohibitive. Emotionally, she anticipates an intensity of love and vulnerability she has not previously experienced; she knows the emotional landscape will change in ways she cannot fully predict. Physically, pregnancy and early parenthood will reshape her body and her sleep in ways that are temporary but not trivial. Her connections will shift: some friendships will deepen through shared parenthood, others will change, the relationship with her husband will be tested and, if navigated well, strengthened. Her identity will be the most significant site of change — she will be a different person, organized differently, with a new and permanent primary relationship that will compete with everything else for her attention, her energy, and her sense of who she is.

Does it truly matter? Yes — this is one of the few decisions in a human life that is genuinely irreversible, and its effects reach into every dimension simultaneously.

How easy is it to reverse? It is not reversible. A child, once born, is a permanent relationship. Parenthood is not a commitment you can examine, try, and walk away from if it turns out to be the wrong fit. The irreversibility is not a reason against it — most of the most valuable things in a life are irreversible, and permanence alone is not a reason to refuse them. But the irreversibility means the clarity required before committing is higher than for a decision that can be revisited. It means the question "is this what I want?" is not sufficient — the question is "is this what I want even on the days when I am exhausted, when the career has had to yield, when the version of myself I built carefully is not quite the version I'm living?"

The path is agency — entered with eyes open to the full picture, including the cost, the permanence, and the fact that the person she will be on the other side of this decision is someone she cannot fully meet in advance. Priya's three years of circling were not avoidance. They were the appropriate weight being given to a decision that deserved it. The path is agency.

Connections is the space between you and other people. The final dimension turns inward — past the body, past the feelings, past the money, past the relationships — to the question that sits beneath all of them: who are you?

IX.

Identity

Who are you?

Who are you beneath the titles, the obligations, and the daily performance of being a person in the world? What do you believe matters? What are you building toward? Does the life you are living belong to the person you actually are, or does it belong to a version of you that was assembled by expectation, circumstance, and the accumulated weight of choices you did not fully make?

Identity is the only dimension that concerns the subject rather than the objects of experience, and the one most people examine last. It sits under the surface of the other four. Your physical habits, your emotional patterns, your financial decisions, your relationships — all of these are shaped by who you believe yourself to be, and all of them, in turn, shape who you are becoming.

This dimension covers your values, your sense of self, your relationship with purpose and meaning, and the stories you tell about yourself. What makes identity distinct from the other four dimensions is that three versions of the self exist simultaneously and can diverge: who you believe yourself to be, who you actually are, and who others take you to be. The gap between any two of these is a source of suffering that no other dimension can locate or address. These are large questions, and they do not lend themselves to easy measurement. You cannot track your identity the way you can track your bank balance or your blood pressure. But you can examine it — candidly, specifically, and with the same questions applied to every other dimension.

Identity is where these questions cut deepest.

The territory is worth mapping before entering it. The core facets are values — what you believe matters, revealed by how you actually live rather than what you say; authenticity — whether who you are and who you present to the world are in alignment; purpose — the direction your effort is pointed; and meaning — the felt sense that your life has significance. These four interact constantly, are often confused with one another, and can produce different paths within the same life. Beyond them are self-concept, life transitions, and cultural identity — each examined in its own section below.

Values

Your values are what you believe matters. Not what you say matters — what you actually live as if it matters, revealed by how you spend your time, your energy, and your attention when no one is watching. Values are the compass. When your life is aligned with them, you feel a coherence that is difficult to name but easy to recognize. When your life is misaligned, you feel a friction that shows up everywhere — in your mood, your motivation, your relationships, your sense that something is off even when nothing visible is wrong.

Most people carry a mix of values they chose and values they absorbed — from family, from culture, from the expectations of the communities they grew up in. The absorbed values may not be yours, and telling the difference is one of the first things the mirror shows you.

The orienting question for values: *If you could design your life from scratch, with no obligations and no audience, what would you keep?*

[C0901] Samuel is fifty-four and has organized his life around a small number of things he cares about deeply: honest work, time with his family, and involvement in his local community. He coaches youth baseball. He volunteers at his church. He runs a plumbing business that earns enough and asks no more of it than that. He turns down opportunities that would require travel or longer hours, because they would cost him time in the places where his values live.

Samuel has never articulated this as a philosophy. He would never describe himself as someone who has "figured out his values." He would say he likes his life, and the liking would be, on examination, the feeling of a life aligned with what he cares about.

Samuel's values are going well — and not by accident. If he applied the orienting question — if he could design his life from scratch, what would he keep? — the answer would look almost exactly like the life he has. The coaching. The community. The plumbing business that earns enough. These are not defaults or compromises. They are the things he would choose again. The coherence between what he believes matters and how he lives is the result of choices he made, some of them costly, including the choice to earn less than he could. The path is appreciation.

[C0902] Nathan is thirty-one and has recently realized that many of the values he has been living by are not his own. He grew up in a family that prized financial success above all else — a family where your worth was measured by your title and your income, where career achievement was the primary topic of conversation, where the cousins who earned the most were held up as examples and the ones who did not were discussed with concern. Nathan absorbed this completely. He pursued a career in finance, earned well, and felt the approval of his family like sunlight.

The problem is that Nathan cares about money differently than his family does. He cares about it enough — he likes comfort, he likes security — but it is not the organizing principle of his life, and living as though it is has produced a persistent hollowness that no raise or promotion has been able to fill. He has been chasing a value that was inherited, not chosen, and the pursuit has crowded out the things he actually cares about: connection, learning, creative work, time spent outside.

Are his values going well? The values he is living by are not his. The values that are his are largely unlived. Does it truly matter? This is the critical question, because the inherited values have produced real rewards — financial stability, family approval, professional status. Nathan must decide whether those rewards are sufficient or whether the hollowness matters more.

On clear examination, the hollowness matters. The rewards are real but hollow. When Nathan applies the orienting question — if he could design his life from scratch, what would he keep? — the finance career is not on the list. The comfort is. The security is. The learning and connection and time outside are.

The career that produces the approval is not. The path is discontinuation of the inherited values he has been living by, and agency directed at building a life organized around what he actually cares about — the values that are his rather than the ones that were absorbed before he knew the difference.

Authenticity

Authenticity is the alignment between who you are and who you show the world. It is related to values but distinct from them — you can have clear values and still be inauthentic if you hide them, perform a version of yourself that contradicts them, or live behind a mask that protects you but also isolates you.

Most people are, to some degree, performing. You present different versions of yourself in different contexts — at work, at home, with friends, with strangers. This is normal and not inherently inauthentic. The question is whether the gap between the performed self and the actual self has grown so wide that you no longer feel known by the people around you. Or whether the performance is costing you something real.

The orienting question for authenticity: *Do the people closest to you know who you actually are?*

[C0903] Fiona is sixty and has arrived, gradually, at a comfort in her own skin that she could not have described at forty. She spent her twenties and thirties performing: the competent professional, the easygoing friend, the daughter her parents wanted. In her forties, she began letting the performance slip — saying what she thought, declining what she did not want, allowing herself to be seen rather than managed. Some relationships ended; they turned out to be built on the performance. The remainder became more real. Is her authenticity going well? Yes. The comfort is not complacency — it is the earned result of becoming visible on her own terms. The path is appreciation.

[C0904] Keiko is forty-two and has been living a double life for as long as she can remember. She grew up in a traditional family with rigid expectations about how a woman should live — marriage, children, deference. She has fulfilled every expectation. She is married, has two children, attends family gatherings, and performs the role with practiced ease.

Inside, she is someone her family has never met. She is intellectually ambitious, deeply political, skeptical of the traditions she was raised in, and privately furious about the constraints she has accepted. She has interests she pursues in secret, opinions she shares with no one in her family, and a sense of self that is invisible to the people who have known her longest.

Is her authenticity going well? No. The gap between who she is and who she presents to her family is enormous, and maintaining it requires constant effort and produces constant friction. Does it truly matter? Yes — the inauthenticity is not a minor social performance. It is a fundamental concealment of who she is from the people closest to her, and the cost is isolation, resentment, and a growing sense that her real self has no place in her own life. Is it in her control to change? Partially, and the partial is where the difficulty lives. She can begin to close the gap — not all at once, and not with the most contested parts of herself first. Agency starts small: sharing a political opinion with one family member she trusts, declining a tradition that contradicts who she is rather than performing it, letting one conversation go unmanaged. These are not declarations. They are openings — small acts that let a little more of her through, that test what the relationship can hold, that give her information about what is possible before she decides how far to go. But she cannot control how her family responds, and the potential consequences — rejection, conflict, rupture — are real.

The path is agency, but agency with significant risk. The mirror does not obscure that risk. What it shows is the cost of continued concealment alongside the cost of visibility — a clear view of what each choice costs. Keiko decides.

Purpose

Purpose is direction — the sense that your effort is pointed somewhere, that what you do today connects to something you are building toward. It is not the same as meaning, though the two are often confused. You can have purpose without meaning — grinding toward a goal that feels hollow — and meaning without purpose — feeling connected and fulfilled, but drifting.

Purpose can be as modest as raising your children well, as concrete as building a business, as quiet as tending a garden that feeds your neighbors. What matters is not the scale of the purpose but whether it is present — whether you wake up with a sense that your effort connects to something you care about, or whether you wake up feeling that the days are passing without trajectory.

The orienting question for purpose: *If someone watched how you spend your weeks, could they tell what you are building toward?*

[C0905] Rosa is forty-nine and runs a small bakery she opened twelve years ago. It pays the bills, supports two employees, and gives the neighborhood a place to sit on Saturday mornings. She knows every regular customer. She develops new recipes in the winter. She takes pride in the craft and in the business as a thing worth maintaining. Rosa's purpose is going well — modest by the world's standards of ambition, exactly right by the standard that matters. The path is appreciation.

[C0906] Diane is forty-seven and built something real. She spent fifteen years growing a nonprofit from a two-person operation into an organization that serves thousands of families. She wrote the grants, hired the staff, shaped the culture, navigated the board politics, and held the mission steady through recessions, leadership crises, and the slow grind of chronic underfunding. The organization bears her imprint more than anyone else's.

Three months ago, the board pushed her out. The reasons were organizational rather than performance-related — a new board chair with a different vision, a funding shift that demanded a different kind of leader, a power struggle she saw coming and could not prevent. She was offered a consultancy role that they both knew was a polite fiction. She declined.

The loss is occupational and purposive — deeper than financial or relational, both of which are holding. The loss is the purpose itself. For fifteen years, she knew what she was building and why. She woke up with direction. She went to bed knowing that her effort had connected to something that mattered — a family that had housing because her organization existed, specific and real, not an abstraction. That connection is gone. The organization continues without her, which is both a credit to what she built and a specific kind of pain.

Diane's first instinct was to start again — to find another nonprofit, another mission, another cause to build around. She began networking, taking meetings, drafting proposals. But something was different. The urgency she expected to feel was not there. In its place was a question she had never had time to ask during the fifteen years of building: is this what I want to do again, or is this what I know how to do?

Is her sense of purpose going well? No. The purpose she carried is gone, and the reflexive reach for a replacement has not produced conviction. Does it truly matter? Yes — the absence is the defining fact of her current life. Is it in her control to change? The obvious answer is yes — she has skills, experience, connections. She could lead another organization within a year. But the questions, asked carefully, reveal that the real issue is not whether she can find new purpose but whether she has been honest about what purpose she actually wants. The nonprofit work was real and mattered. It was also consuming — it absorbed her identity so completely that she does not know, at forty-seven, what she cares about apart from it. The question is not "can I rebuild?" The question is "should I rebuild the same thing, or is this the moment to discover what else is there?"

The path is agency, but a slower and more honest form of agency than Diane's instincts suggest. Not the immediate agency of finding the next role. The deeper agency of sitting with the discomfort long enough to discover whether her purpose is a specific cause or something she has not yet named.

Meaning

Meaning is the sense that your life matters — that what you do, who you are, and how you spend your time has significance beyond the immediate. It is not the same as purpose, though they often travel together. Purpose is directional: you are building toward something. Meaning is experiential: you feel that what you are doing connects to something beyond yourself — beyond this task, this day, this individual effort.

Meaning comes from many sources — from love, from work, from contribution, from faith, from the simple accumulation of a life lived with attention. It cannot be manufactured or purchased or optimized into existence. It tends to arrive as a byproduct of engagement rather than as a goal pursued directly.

The orienting question for meaning: *Does your life feel like it matters to you — not to an audience, not on paper, but in the living of it?*

[C0907] Patricia is fifty-three and finds meaning in places that would not make a list of important things. She finds it in cooking dinner for her family — because the act of feeding the people she loves is, for her, a small daily expression of care that accumulates into something substantial. She finds it in her garden, in the satisfaction of tending something alive, and in her work as a school librarian, where the meaning is not in the title or the pay but in the specific moments — a reluctant reader who finds the right book, a teenager who needs a quiet place and knows hers is available.

Patricia does not describe her life as meaningful. But the mirror, held up to her daily experience, shows a life saturated with small significances that together produce something real.

Is her sense of meaning going well? Yes. Not through grand purpose or transcendent experience, but through the accumulated texture of a life lived with attention. The path is appreciation.

She is fifty-three. The school where she works will not need her forever, and she knows it — budgets tighten, libraries are consolidated, the role she has occupied with quiet competence for eighteen years is the kind that institutions eliminate without ceremony. Her children are grown. The cooking will outlast the career. The garden does not require a title.

This is what makes Patricia's case philosophically useful: she will not face a post-work identity crisis, not because her career is secure, but because her meaning was never housed there. The crisis that unmoors people when work ends — the sudden vacancy where purpose used to be — arrives most brutally for people who built their meaning exclusively inside the role. Patricia built hers in the texture of daily life, and the texture will remain when the role is gone. The path is appreciation — and the appreciation worth naming here is not only for what she has, but for the way she came to have it: by paying attention to the right things, before circumstances forced the question.

[C0908] Colin is forty-four and has looked carefully. His search is genuine. He examines his daily life — his work, which he finds neither satisfying nor meaningful; his evenings, which he fills without particular enjoyment; his weekends, which pass without leaving a mark — and finds them genuinely empty. Not compared to some imagined version of a meaningful life. Empty in that nothing in them produces the sense that any of it matters.

He is not depressed in the clinical sense — his sleep is normal, his functioning is intact, he is not in pain, and he takes pleasure in small things. He is empty in a quieter way: a life that goes through the motions without generating the sense that the motions are connected to anything that counts. He has tried the things people suggest. He volunteers occasionally; it produces satisfaction in the moment that does not persist. He has tried new hobbies; they engage him without gripping him. He has a relationship that works without feeling essential. Nothing has taken hold.

Is his sense of meaning going well? No — the absence is genuine, not manufactured and not a product of measuring against the wrong standard. Does it truly matter? Yes. The absence is real and persistent and affects his experience of being alive. Is it in his control to change? He does not yet know, because he has not yet done the work that might reveal it. The path is agency, but a specific kind — the deeper agency of examining where meaning has come from for people like him, rather than reaching for another hobby or volunteer shift. This kind of emptiness often has roots in the values and authenticity facets: a life that is not aligned with what the person actually cares about, or a self that has not been examined closely enough to know what it cares about. Colin's work is to find out who he is on the inside — and that work, when it is this persistent and this unresponsive to ordinary effort, is often best done with professional help. The path is agency: not the agency of finding a new hobby, but the deeper agency of examining what he actually values and how he actually lives — the kind of inquiry that requires real effort and often requires someone else to help hold the mirror. The emptiness is real, it matters, and the examination that would address it has not yet been done.

[C0909] Josephine is sixty-one and has attended the same church for thirty-four years. Her faith is not a hobby or a habit. It is the organizing structure of her inner life — the thing she turns to first when something goes wrong and the thing she is most grateful for when something goes right. She prays daily, as conversation. She reads scripture for orientation — the way a sailor checks the stars, not because the stars tell you where to go but because they tell you where you are.

Her faith has not been untested. She lost her husband to cancer eleven years ago. She raised two children alone on a teacher's salary. She has watched friends leave the church over disagreements she understands and partly shares. She has had her own seasons of doubt — stretches where the prayers felt hollow, where the comfort she expected did not arrive, where she wondered whether the structure she had built her life around was something she had chosen or something she had inherited and never questioned.

She questioned it. The answer, each time, was that the faith was hers. The life it produced was the life she recognized as her own — that was reason enough, more durable than proof, more honest than the doubts that had never fully resolved. The community, the practice, the sense of participating in something larger and older than herself, the framework for understanding suffering that did not require suffering to be meaningless — these were not inherited obligations she had failed to examine. They were examined, tested, shaken, and still standing.

Is her relationship with faith going well? Yes. It sustains her, orients her, and gives her daily life a dimension of significance that extends beyond what she can see or measure. The path is appreciation.

Self-Concept

Your self-concept is the story you tell about who you are — the roles you play, the traits you assign yourself, and the narrative you have built about your life. It matters because it acts as a filter. It determines what you attempt, what you avoid, and what you believe is possible for you. A person who sees herself as resilient interprets setbacks differently from a person who sees herself as fragile.

The orienting question for self-concept: *Does the story you tell about yourself match who you actually are?*

[C0910] Ruben is thirty-three and still sees himself as the shy kid. The label was applied in childhood — by his parents, who described him to others as "the quiet one," by teachers who noted his reluctance to speak in class, by a social environment that treated introversion as a deficit. Ruben internalized it completely. He is, at thirty-three, organized around the belief that he is fundamentally shy — a belief that shapes his career choices, his social behavior, and his expectations for himself.

The problem is that the label no longer fits. Ruben is not the child he was. He has learned to speak publicly and does it well. He has friendships that are engaged and reciprocal. He runs a team at work and manages conflict without difficulty. By any external observation, he is not shy. But the self-concept persists, and it costs him: he declines opportunities that require visibility, he undermines his own contributions in meetings, and he carries a baseline assumption that he is less capable socially than the evidence suggests.

Is his self-concept going well? No — he is carrying an outdated story about himself that no longer matches who he is. Does it truly matter? Yes — the outdated label is constraining his career, his social life, and his sense of what is possible. The path is discontinuation — release the old label. "Shy" was an assessment made about a child by people who did not know the adult he would become. Carrying it at thirty-three is carrying weight that does not belong to him. The path is discontinuation: the energy currently spent organizing his life around an identity that no longer fits can be redirected toward living as the person he actually is.

[C0911] Vivian is forty-five and has built her entire career on proving people wrong. She grew up in a family that did not take her seriously — the youngest of four, the only girl, told repeatedly in ways both direct and subtle that she was not as capable as her brothers. She absorbed the message, and then she weaponized it. She was the first in her family to finish college. She built a business from nothing. She outearned all three brothers by the time she was thirty-five. Every achievement was accompanied by a private satisfaction: a score settled, a debt repaid, proof delivered to people who had underestimated her.

The chip on her shoulder was fuel. It got her through the years when the business was failing, when the money was not there, when a more contented person would have stopped. It gave her a reason to keep going that had nothing to do with the work itself and everything to do with the story she was living inside: I will show them.

She showed them. And now, at forty-five, the chip is still there — but the audience is gone. Her parents are elderly and proud of her. Her brothers have long since stopped competing. The people she was proving wrong have either changed their minds or faded from her life. The grievance that organized her ambition for twenty years no longer has an object. And yet it persists. She still works as though someone is watching and doubting, and still cannot enjoy a success without measuring it against the old wound. She still carries a combativeness in meetings, in negotiations, in friendships, that people around her experience as exhausting even when they admire her competence.

Is her self-concept going well? No. The identity built around the grievance was useful once and is costly now. It produces drive without satisfaction, achievement without rest, and a defensiveness that is damaging her relationships. Does it truly matter? Yes — the cost is real and growing. Her marriage is strained by a competitiveness she brings home. Her employees respect her but do not trust her with vulnerability. She is tired in a way that has nothing to do with hours. Is it in her control to change? The chip was a response to something real — the dismissal was genuine, and the anger was proportionate at the time. But the response has outlasted the cause.

The path is discontinuation — not of the drive, which is hers to keep, but of the grievance that fuels it. The question is whether the drive can outlast the grievance.

[C0912] Alicia is forty-nine and has a file of performance reviews that say the same thing, year after year: exceeds expectations. Her manager praises her thoroughness, her reliability, her ability to deliver under pressure. Five years at the same company, five reviews that any reasonable person would be proud of. Alicia is not proud of them. She barely reads them anymore.

What she reads instead is the list of annual award recipients, which has never included her name, and the promotion announcements, which have included the names of three peers who started after she did. She watches these colleagues recognized in company meetings — applauded, congratulated, advanced — and each time something tightens in her chest. She has rehearsed quitting in her mind dozens of times. She has drafted resignation letters she did not send. She lies awake some nights composing arguments to her manager that she will not deliver. The job itself is fine. The work is fine. Her performance is, by her organization's own repeated assessment, excellent. None of this registers. The reviews arrive and produce nothing — no satisfaction, no steadiness, no sense that she is doing well — because they are measured against the wrong benchmark.

The mirror splits what looks like one problem into several.

Her performance: is it going well? Yes. Five years of high reviews is not ambiguous. The path is appreciation — and this is where Alicia has the most work to do, because the appreciation cannot land. She has evidence that she is good at her job, delivered repeatedly by the people who evaluate her, and she has made it worthless by treating it as a consolation prize for the thing she did not get. The first question is answered — and she will not accept the answer.

The promotion: is it going well? No. Does it truly matter? Yes — it carries compensation, scope, and professional standing that are concrete. Is it in her control? This is the question she has not asked clearly. Five years without promotion despite excellent reviews is a signal, and the signal has two possible meanings: either the barrier is structural — no openings, political dynamics, a manager who values her in her current role too much to advocate for moving her out of it — or the barrier is a gap she has not identified between what she is doing and what a promotion requires. She does not know which one it is, because she has been too busy being wounded to investigate. The path is agency — the agency of finding out what is actually in her way, before quitting becomes the conclusion. A direct conversation with her manager about the specific criteria for promotion. An honest assessment of whether this organization will ever promote her or whether the ceiling is real. If the ceiling is real, agency shifts to a job search — not a rage quit but a strategic move informed by clarity about what she wants and what this place cannot give her.

The awards: is this going well? No. Does it truly matter? Here the mirror surfaces the question Alicia has not separated from the promotion. If she were promoted tomorrow, would the absence of awards still hurt? If the answer is no, the awards do not independently matter — they were a proxy for advancement, and the path is discontinuation. If the answer is yes, what she needs is not an award but proof that she is seen, and that need lives deeper than any plaque or ceremony can reach.

The path is agency — toward pursuing a promotion or finding a new job.

Life Transitions

There are moments in life when your identity is forced to reorganize — when the story you have been telling about yourself no longer fits, and a new one must be built whether you are ready or not. These moments are life transitions: becoming a parent, losing a parent, retirement, divorce, job loss, a diagnosis that changes what your body can do, a coming out that changes how you are seen. Some transitions are events. Others are slower: the seventy-year-old who finds that the assumptions he built his life on — about work, about gender, about community — are no longer shared by the world around him. His identity as the competent elder feels newly irrelevant, and acceptance, rather than resistance to it, is the path forward.

Transitions are events rather than ongoing territories of your identity, sometimes chosen and sometimes forced, that crack the existing identity open and require something new to form in its place. They belong in this chapter because the transition breaks the story, and the broken story forces the question: who am I now?

[C0913] Grant is fifty-two and has been laid off from a company where he worked for nineteen years. He did not see it coming. He went to work on a Tuesday and was told, by early afternoon, that his position had been eliminated. He was walked to his car with a box of personal items and a severance package that did not come close to matching what he had given.

Grant's identity was built on his career. Not just his job — his career: the title, the expertise, the network, the sense that he was someone who mattered in a specific context. Without the context, the someone feels undefined. He wakes up with nowhere to go and no one expecting him, and the formlessness of his days is not liberating. It is terrifying.

Is the transition going well? No. His identity has been destabilized by the loss of the role that organized it, and the destabilization is affecting his mood, his confidence, and his sense of who he is. Does it truly matter? Yes — this is not a minor disruption. Is it in his control to change? The layoff is not — it happened and cannot be undone. But the identity crisis it triggered is addressable. Grant can find new work, and the job search is a form of agency. More importantly, he can examine whether his identity should have been so dependent on a single role, and whether the identity he builds going forward might be broader, more resilient, and less vulnerable to the decisions of a company. The answer is agency for the practical recovery and for the deeper identity work.

Cultural and Social Identity

There is a layer of identity that is not chosen but assigned — by the society you were born into, by the body you inhabit, by the categories the world uses to sort people before they have spoken a word. Race, gender, sexuality, religion, ethnicity, class, disability — these are identities that shape your experience whether you have examined them or not, and they interact with every other facet of identity in ways that can be difficult to disentangle.

The orienting question: *How much of who you believe yourself to be was chosen by you, and how much was assigned?*

Cultural and social identity affects how you are seen, what is expected of you, what doors open and which ones resist, how much of your identity is yours to define and how much was defined for you before you arrived. These assigned identities may align with your experience and require little examination, or they may be the source of fundamental conflict — between who you are and who the world insists you should be, between the identity you carry internally and the one projected onto you externally.

The questions apply here, but they require particular care, because much of what falls under cultural and social identity is not within your control. You cannot choose your race, your place of birth, or the social categories that shape how the world treats you. What you can choose, to varying degrees, is how you carry these identities — whether you accept them, resist them, integrate them, or redefine them. The interplay between what is assigned and what is chosen is one of the deepest questions this dimension raises, and the mirror can help you see it clearly, even if it cannot resolve it.

Two identities coexist in this dimension: the one others assign to you, and the one you hold for yourself. These sometimes align. Often they do not. A person may be seen by the world as one thing — defined by skin color, by accent, by disability, by gender — while experiencing themselves as something far more specific and complex than the category allows. The gap between assigned identity and internal identity is not a problem to be solved. It is a permanent condition of living in a society that sorts people into groups, and the questions can help you determine where that gap matters, where it does not, and what part of it is within your control to address.

Other Facets

Other facets of identity include your relationship with mortality, questions of legacy, the gap between your public self and your private self, identity shaped by major life experiences such as military service, and the ongoing negotiation between who you were, who you are, and who you are becoming. Each can be examined with the same questions.

The Past: What Happened in This Dimension, and How Should I Carry It?

Did it go well? Did it truly matter? Is there anything still in my control to change?

The identity past is the most interior of the five dimensions' pasts. In the financial dimension, what you carry from the past is a changed position — calculable, present, affecting your numbers. In the connections dimension, it is an absence — a person or relationship no longer there. In identity, what you carry is a story: the person you believed yourself to be, or were becoming, or failed to become. The past question set asks whether that story is still accurate, still useful, and still yours to carry.

Two things are worth examining in the identity past: the aspirations that did not come true, and the selves you have genuinely left behind. Both require a kind of release — but the release looks different in each case, and confusing them is how this dimension often stays unexamined.

[C0914] Elena is fifty-three and has been painting since she was nineteen. Not as a pastime — as a life. She got an MFA at twenty-four. She showed in galleries in her late twenties and early thirties. She was told by people whose judgment she respected that her work was good. She believed them, and she organized her identity around what she expected to follow: a career, a body of work shown and discussed and collected, a livelihood that came from the thing she made.

The career did not materialize. Not suddenly — there was no single rejection, no defining failure, no moment when the door visibly closed. It accumulated, the way these things do: the galleries became harder to access, the grants were awarded to others, the shows thinned, the buyers did not appear in sufficient numbers. The rent did not thin. At thirty-nine she took an administrative job at a design firm. The job became a career. At forty-five she was a department head. She is, by most accounts, successful.

She still paints. Evenings, weekends, a longer stretch in the summers when her schedule allows. The work has not stopped. What has stopped is the public life of the work — the shows, the recognition, the income, the professional identity. She is a painter who is not a painter in the way she planned to be.

Did the aspiration go well? No — the career she organized her identity around in her twenties and thirties did not come true. Did it truly matter? Yes. This was not a casual ambition. It was the definition of who she understood herself to be, held for more than two decades, and the gap between what she expected and what arrived is real and still present. Is there anything in her control to change? The career she imagined — shows, livelihood, recognition at scale — is, at fifty-three, behind her. The path she did not take is closed.

The path is acceptance — but precisely drawn. What she is releasing is a specific form of her work's life in the world: the career, the professional identity, the public version of the painter she expected to become. She is not releasing the practice or the work. She is not even releasing the showing of it — local exhibitions, smaller venues, the particular audience available to her — if those still matter to her. What acceptance asks her to release is the belief that the career that did not arrive is still the right story for who she is. At fifty-three, it is not. The painter she is — the one who has made work for thirty years, whose practice has deepened through two decades of evenings and summers — is the painter she actually is, not a consolation prize for the painter she expected to be. The path is acceptance of that fact, and it is not a small thing.

[C0915] Thomas is forty-six and is no longer the person he was at twenty-four. At twenty-four, he was devout — deeply, specifically, organizingly devout, in a tradition that structured his days, his relationships, and his judgments of other people. The faith was genuine. So were the views it produced: he believed, with conviction and without much examination, that people who lived differently from the way his tradition prescribed were living wrongly. He ended a friendship because of how that friend loved. He said things to his parents and to his younger sister about their choices that came from that belief system and caused genuine harm. He was not, by his own current assessment, a cruel person. He was a certain person, and certainty at twenty-four, in a tradition that answered every question, produced real damage.

He left the tradition at thirty-one. Not in crisis — gradually, through reading, through relationships, through the slow accumulation of evidence that the framework he had accepted whole was partial. He revised. The revision was genuine and complete. He does not hold the views he held at twenty-four. He has not held them for fifteen years. He is, by any reasonable measure, a different person on these questions.

And yet he carries the guilt — persistently, as a low-level self-prosecution that has followed him from his thirties into his forties, shaping how he sees himself and what he believes he deserves. It surfaces in his closest relationships, where he tends to over-explain his current beliefs as though his past self might otherwise contaminate the present one. It surfaces in political and social conversations, where he is thorough to the point of exhaustion in renouncing what he used to believe. The guilt has become its own kind of identity: the person who did real harm and will not let himself forget it.

Did it go well? No. The views he held caused real harm to real people who deserved better. Did it truly matter? Yes — the friendship that ended has not resumed. The things he said to his sister still live in the years between them, acknowledged but unresolved in the way that some things between siblings stay unresolved even after the words have been said. Is there anything in his control to change?

Here the mirror makes a cut. Some things remain open. The friendship is untested — the same situation Ian was in: a possibility treated as a confirmed outcome without ever being tried. The agency is real. The conversation with his sister about what was said between them has not been had in full, and it belongs to him to initiate. These are genuine agencies. This guilt is proportionate — it points to something that can still be addressed.

Other things are not open. The views themselves are gone. The person who held them is not the person Thomas is now, and has not been for fifteen years. The guilt that attaches to that past self — the guilt that persists after the repair has been attempted, after the apology has been made, after the self has genuinely changed — is no longer doing the work of conscience. It is doing something else: keeping him organized around an identity he has left, prosecuting a self that no longer exists. That guilt belongs to a self that no longer exists.

The path is split. Agency for what remains open — the friendship not yet attempted, the conversation not yet fully had. Discontinuation for the guilt attached to a self that has genuinely been revised: not because the harm was minor, but because prosecuting a person who no longer exists repairs nothing. It only prevents the person who has changed from living as though the change is real. The path is discontinuation of the guilt, and agency in the relationships still open.

The Future: What Has Not Yet Happened, and How Should I Enter It?

How will this affect the five dimensions? Does this truly matter? How easy is it to reverse if I change my mind?

The identity dimension is where future questions carry the most personal weight. A decision to change careers, return to school, pursue a deferred creative commitment — these are not only financial or logistical questions. They are questions about who you are becoming. And the third question — how easy is it to reverse? — applies to the practical decision and to the identity itself: once you step into a different kind of life, you become, in some part, a different kind of person. That too is not fully reversible.

The future question set, applied here, does one specific thing that ordinary deliberation does not: it separates what is genuinely at stake from the anxiety that surrounds every decision of this kind.

[C0916] Rachel is forty-one and has spent fifteen years in marketing. She is good at it — recognized, well compensated, with a career that has progressed in the ways careers are supposed to. She is also, with increasing certainty, finished with it. Not burned out: finished. The work is competent and empty in equal measure, and the emptiness has been growing for several years.

What she wants to do — has wanted for longer than she has admitted — is environmental law. Not vaguely: she has researched programs, identified the three schools she would apply to, taken the LSAT twice, and scored well enough to have realistic prospects at each of them. The research is done. The application is drafted and not sent. What has not happened is the decision.

The obstacle is not information. It is the pressure surrounding the decision — a formless urgency that sounds like "before it is too late" and that she cannot distinguish from the sober recognition that forty-one is a real number and the pivot gets harder the longer she waits.

The future questions cut through the pressure.

How will this affect the five dimensions? Financially, law school means three years of tuition and reduced income — substantial, and she has modeled it. The career on the other side pays less than her current one, at least initially; the work she imagines doing does not optimize for compensation. She has savings and no dependents. The financial picture is demanding and manageable. Emotionally, the decision carries the grief of leaving something she built and the fear of beginning again as a beginner. The emotional dimension will be harder than the financial one. Physically, three years of school at forty-one is not the same as at twenty-four; she knows this and has made peace with the desk hours and the particular exhaustion of being the older student in the room. Her connections will shift: the professional network she has built over fifteen years in marketing will not transfer, and she will spend years building one in a field that does not yet know her. Her identity is where the change is largest — she will not be a marketing executive who wanted to be an environmental lawyer. She will be an environmental lawyer. The shift is an identity change — deeper than a credential, and she knows it.

Does it truly matter? Yes. Three years of examination have produced a sustained, specific conviction that the work she is doing and the work she wants to do are different, and that the difference matters enough to cost what it will cost. The importance is genuine, not manufactured by anxiety.

How easy is it to reverse? Admission to a program is reversible — withdrawing before the first semester costs only the application. The first year costs more: time, money, the beginning of an identity shift. By the third year, the identity cost of not finishing outweighs the cost of finishing. The window for easy reversal is narrow and is at the beginning, before the commitment deepens. That is where she is now.

The path is agency. Not because the decision is easy — the financial cost is real, the emotional disruption is real, and the career she is leaving will not wait for her if she changes her mind. But the examination has produced what anxiety alone does not: a clear picture of what is actually at stake, separated from what merely feels urgent. What is actually at stake is a life organized around work she cares about, entered through a specific and available door, at a cost she has modeled and accepted. The "now or never" pressure, examined, turns out to be approximately correct: forty-one is a real number, the pivot is available now in a way it will not be indefinitely, and the urgency, in this case, is not anxiety wearing the costume of importance. It is importance. The path is agency.

But life does not always sort itself neatly into one dimension at a time.

PART III:

THE HARDER CASES

X.

When the Picture Is Not Clear

This chapter assumes familiarity with the four paths, the five dimensions, facets, and the questions for the past, present, and future. This chapter builds on them.

The earlier chapters examined one facet at a time. This chapter turns to the harder situations: sources that live in a different dimension than the symptom, paths that conflict, answers that change over time, and cases where the question itself resists a clear answer.

These are the gray areas — where the source is hard to find, where multiple dimensions are involved simultaneously, where the boundary between agency and acceptance is blurred, where the answer you arrived at last year no longer fits, or where time itself is part of the difficulty.

What does not change is the mirror itself. The paths, question sets, and dimensions remain unchanged. Complex situations call for rigorous analysis — specifically, the work of locating which dimension holds the source, which may not be the dimension where the pain is felt. Apply the questions where the pain is felt. If the path resolves the suffering, the source is there. If it does not, apply them in the next dimension and continue until the source reveals itself.

This chapter walks through several extended cases — longer and more detailed than those in the dimension chapters — because the process of working through that analysis is the point. In a clean case, the mirror produces an answer quickly. In a gray area, the questions must be applied multiple times, in multiple dimensions, before the picture becomes clear. For gray areas especially, pen and paper can help — writing out each question and its answer as you move through the dimensions makes the iteration easier to track.

Finding the Source

The life behind it has gone quiet.

[C1001] Marta is forty-three and has been depressed for two years. She feels a constant weight that will not lift. She has less energy than she used to. She takes less pleasure in things she used to enjoy. She has slowly withdrawn from friends, finding reasons to cancel plans and not making new ones. She functions — she goes to work, she takes care of her children, she meets her obligations — but the functioning is mechanical. The life behind it has gone quiet.

Marta's first assumption is that this is an emotional problem. Depression is, after all, an emotional experience. She begins there — examines her emotional baseline, asks whether it is going well (it is not), whether it matters (it does), and whether it is in her control to change. She sees a therapist. She tries medication. Both help modestly — the edges soften, the worst days become less frequent — but the core flatness remains. After six months of treatment, she is better but not well, and she begins to wonder whether she is looking in the right place.

She examines the physical dimension. Her sleep is adequate. Her health is stable. She exercises sporadically but has no physical complaints. The physical dimension is not the source.

She examines the financial dimension. She and her husband earn enough. They are not in debt. There is no financial pressure that could account for the flatness. This dimension is not the source either.

She examines connections. Her marriage is functional. Her children are healthy. Her friendships have suffered, but the withdrawal feels like a consequence of the depression rather than its cause — she pulled away because she did not have the energy to show up, not because the relationships themselves were failing.

She examines identity. And here, something shifts.

Marta went to law school because her parents expected it. She practiced law for three years, hated it, and left to become a teacher — a decision that produced a rupture with her family that has never fully healed. She has been teaching for fourteen years. She is good at it. She used to love it. But when she is honest — truly honest, in the way the mirror asks — she realizes that she has not loved it for several years. The work has become routine. The meaning she once found in it has faded. And the deeper issue, the one she has not wanted to face, is that she became a teacher partly as a reaction against her parents' expectations, which means the choice was not entirely hers — it was a rejection of their values rather than an affirmation of her own. She does not know what she would choose if she were choosing freely, and the not knowing has been sitting beneath her life for years.

The depression is real. The emotional experience is real. But the source is in the identity dimension — a life organized around a reaction rather than a choice, producing a creeping loss of meaning that eventually manifested as flatness. The therapy and medication addressed the emotional symptoms, which is why they helped at the margins. They did not address the source, which is why the core flatness remained.

The questions, applied to the right dimension: Is her sense of purpose and meaning going well? No — it has eroded over years, and the erosion predates the depression. Does it truly matter? Yes — the loss of meaning in the central activity of her life is not a minor issue. Is it in her control to change? Yes. She cannot undo the years she spent teaching as a reaction, but she can examine what she would choose if she were choosing now, and she can begin to build toward it. The path is agency in the identity dimension. The depression may lift as a consequence — or it may require continued treatment alongside the identity work. Both the symptom and the source deserve attention.

The Cascade

It feels like everything went wrong at once.

[C1002] Kevin is fifty-one and his life is coming apart in every direction at once. His back went out eight months ago — a disc problem that required surgery, followed by a recovery that has been slower and more painful than he was told to expect. He is still in pain most days. During the recovery, he could not work for three months, and the lost income put pressure on finances that were already tight. The financial pressure produced arguments with his wife — not about money specifically, but about everything, the way financial strain does, turning small disagreements into referendums on the relationship. The arguments have eroded the ease between them. He feels distant from her. He has stopped seeing friends because he does not want to explain the situation, and the isolation has darkened his mood. He used to think of himself as capable, independent, and strong. He now thinks of himself as broken, dependent, and diminished. Every dimension of his life is affected. The question is: where did it start?

When Kevin looks at the cascade — health declining, finances strained, marriage tense, social life collapsed, identity shaken — it feels like everything went wrong at once.

The origin, in Kevin's case, is physical. The back injury is the event that set the cascade in motion. The lost income was a direct consequence of the injury. The marital tension was a consequence of the financial pressure, which was a consequence of the injury. The social withdrawal was a consequence of the pain and the mood, both of which trace back to the injury. The identity crisis — the shift from capable to broken — is the furthest downstream consequence, but it too began with a body that stopped cooperating.

This matters because it changes where the effort goes. Kevin has been trying to fix his marriage, which feels like the most urgent problem. But the marriage was fine before the injury, and the marital tension is a downstream effect of physical injury — the relationship is strained because of the injury and the financial strain it produced. He has been trying to restore his self-image, which feels like the deepest problem. But his self-image was stable before the injury, and it will stabilize again when the cascade is addressed at its root.

The questions, applied at the origin: Is his physical well-being going well? No — the pain is persistent and limiting. Does it truly matter? Yes — it has triggered a cascade that reaches every dimension of his life. Is it in his control to change? Partially.

The surgery is done, and the recovery trajectory is partly beyond his control. But pain management, physical therapy, and a realistic timeline for returning to work are all facets of agency. The path is agency for what he can address in the physical dimension, and acceptance for the recovery timeline he cannot accelerate.

The cascade analysis reveals that if Kevin addresses the physical root, several downstream effects may resolve on their own. The financial pressure eases when he returns to work. The marital tension eases when the financial pressure lifts and when he is no longer in daily pain. The social withdrawal eases when his mood improves. The identity crisis eases when he can function again.

Not all cascades are this traceable. Some have multiple origins. Some have loops — the pain causes the depression, the depression reduces the motivation to do physical therapy, the missed therapy slows the recovery, the slow recovery increases the pain. When a cascade loops, the entry point for agency may be wherever the loop is most breakable rather than wherever it began. Kevin's loop might be best broken at the physical therapy point — the one place where consistent effort has the most chance of interrupting the cycle. The mirror shows you the full picture so you can choose the one that is most likely to work.

Partial Control

She never knows, on any given morning, which kind of day it will be.

[C1003] Catherine is thirty-eight and has rheumatoid arthritis. The disease is progressive, unpredictable, and incurable. Some days she functions well — the medication manages the inflammation, her joints cooperate. Other days, she cannot open a jar or climb stairs without pain. She never knows, on any given morning, which kind of day it will be.

The challenge is that agency and acceptance coexist in the same facet, sometimes in the same hour. Within her control: medication, physical therapy, stress management, sleep, adjusting her schedule on bad days. Not within her control: whether the disease progresses, the vagaries of when a flare arrives, whether new damage accumulates despite her best efforts. Between these two lists is a gray area — the daily decisions about when to push and when to rest, when to fight through the pain and when to honor it. These decisions are not purely agency and not purely acceptance. They are partial control, and partial control is where a big part of life actually lives.

The questions help, but they must be asked with specificity. "Is my arthritis in my control?" is too large — the answer is both yes and no. "Can I show up for physical therapy three times a week?" — yes, and the path is agency. "Will the disease spare my daughter's recital?" — no, and the path is acceptance. "Can I ask for help on the days my hands will not cooperate?" — yes, and the path is agency. The mirror works here through repeated application at close range, arriving at a mosaic of paths rather than a single answer.

The Answer That Changes

What was acceptance is now, potentially, agency again.

[C1004] Michael is forty-five and accepted, five years ago, that his marriage was over. The acceptance came slowly, through an accumulation of evidence that the relationship, despite years of effort, was not going to become what either of them needed. He and his wife had tried therapy, structured date nights, separate hobbies and shared projects — everything the marriage counselor and the books and the well-meaning friends had suggested. Nothing changed the fundamental reality: they had grown into different people, and those people did not fit together the way they had once fit together.

The acceptance was painful but clarifying. Michael stopped fighting. He stopped hoping that the next effort would be the one that worked. He settled into the marriage as it was — functional, cordial, cooperative as coparents, and empty of the intimacy that both of them once expected it to contain. He accepted this as the cost of stability, of the children's well-being, of the practical architecture of a shared life.

And then something changed that he did not expect. His wife, independently and without his knowledge, began her own process of examination — prompted, as it happened, by a health scare that forced her to reconsider everything. She arrived at conclusions about the marriage that were similar to his but led her to a different response. She wanted to try again — not with the old methods, which had failed, but with a new therapist, a new approach, and a willingness to be vulnerable that she had not shown before. She told Michael this, and he found himself facing a situation that had unexpectedly changed.

The questions, revisited: Is the marriage going well? No — it has been in a state of cordial emptiness for five years. Does it truly matter? Yes — it is still the central relationship in his life. Is it in his control to change? This is where the answer has shifted. Five years ago, the answer was no — he had exhausted his agency, and his wife was not willing to engage. Now, her willingness has changed, and with it, the boundary between agency and acceptance has moved. What was acceptance is now, potentially, agency again.

Michael does not have to act on this. Acceptance, once genuinely reached, is not easily reversed, and the self-protection it provides is real. Reopening the effort means reopening the possibility of failure, of hope followed by another disappointment, of a cycle he worked hard to exit. But it may also lead to a revitalized relationship. The choice is his. The mirror shows him what is true: the situation has changed, the previous assessment no longer fits, and the questions, applied to the current reality, produce a different path than they did five years ago. What was acceptance is now, potentially, agency again. What he does with that information is his.

♦ ◇ ♦

The Problem That Sprawls

If she is not the high-performing professional, who is she?

[C1005] Rebecca is forty and burned out. Not exhausted — burned out, which is a different thing entirely. Exhaustion can be fixed with enough rest. Burnout cannot be fixed with rest and it can span multiple dimensions.

Her body is exhausted — she sleeps poorly, eats irregularly, and has had three colds in four months. Emotionally, she is flat;

she cries in her car before work, composes herself, and performs through the day. Financially, she earns well, but the earning is the trap — she has built a lifestyle that depends on the job that is destroying her. Her connections have withered; her partner gets the remnants of her energy, and her friends have stopped calling. And beneath it all: she does not know who she is outside of work. Her career has been the organizing principle of her identity for fifteen years, and the career is now the thing she cannot sustain.

If she is not the high-performing professional, who is she? The question is terrifying enough that she avoids it.

Every dimension is affected. Where is the root?

Rebecca's burnout accumulated across all dimensions simultaneously, each reinforcing the others in a self-sustaining cycle. The exhaustion reduces her capacity to address the emotional flatness. The flatness reduces her motivation to escape the financial trap. The trap keeps her in the job. The job perpetuates the exhaustion. And the identity question prevents her from imagining her way out.

When the source is everywhere, the mirror asks a different question: where is the cycle most breakable?

For Rebecca, the answer is identity — specifically, the identity question is preventing all the others from being addressed. She cannot solve the financial trap without imagining a different career. She cannot imagine a different career without confronting who she is beyond the current one. The identity dimension is the lock, and the other dimensions are the doors it is keeping closed.

The questions, applied to identity: Is her sense of self going well? No — it has been reduced to a single role that is failing. Does it truly matter? Yes — the reduction is the core of the burnout. Is it in her control to change? Yes, though the timing and capacity matter.

Rebecca cannot do deep identity work while she is running on empty — burnout reduces the very cognitive and emotional resources that self-examination requires. The first act of agency may not be the identity work itself but the creation of enough breathing room to make the identity work possible: a leave of absence, a reduction in hours, a temporary lowering of standards that her current self-concept will resist. She can begin examining who she is beyond the career — not to abandon it immediately, but to build enough identity outside it that the career no longer holds the full weight of her self-concept. This is slow, uncomfortable work, and it is what makes everything else accessible.

The path is agency — leading to multiple actions, in sequence. Agency in the physical dimension first: rest, reduced hours, breathing room — the identity question cannot be answered by a person running on empty.

When the Paths Conflict

Sometimes the mirror produces a clear answer in one dimension that directly contradicts the clear answer in another. Not a cascade, not a blurred root — a genuine conflict, where following the right path in one dimension requires accepting a cost in another.

Both answers are honest.

[C1006] Naomi is forty-four and has been offered a promotion that would double her salary and require her to relocate across the country. She is a single mother of two teenagers. Her finances are tight — constrained in ways that limit her options and produce a low-grade stress she has carried for years. The promotion would eliminate that stress entirely. It would fund her children's education. It would give her a financial cushion she has never had. In the financial dimension, the questions are unambiguous: her financial well-being is not going well, it truly matters, and the promotion is within her control to accept. The path in the financial dimension is agency.

But the promotion requires leaving the city where her children have grown up, where their father lives and shares custody, where their friends and schools and sense of stability are rooted. Her older daughter is sixteen and in the middle of high school. Her younger son is thirteen and already struggling with the upheaval of adolescence. When Naomi examines the connections dimension, the picture is equally clear but points in the opposite direction: her children's stability is going well, it truly matters, and uprooting them is within her control — which means protecting their stability is also within her control. The path in the connections dimension is appreciation: see what is working and protect it.

Financial agency says: take the promotion. Relational appreciation says: protect what your children have. Both answers are honest. Both are the product of the questions applied correctly. And they are incompatible.

The mirror surfaces this conflict clearly. The relative weight of dimensions is personal — it depends on your values, your circumstances, and what you are willing to trade. Naomi is not facing a vague sense of being "torn." She is facing a specific tradeoff: financial agency at the cost of disruption to her children's connections, or protection of those connections at the cost of continued financial constraint.

What Naomi decides depends on factors the mirror can show but cannot weigh. How resilient are her children? How severe is the financial constraint? Is the promotion a one-time opportunity or the kind of offer that will come again? Could she negotiate a delayed start, a remote arrangement, a compromise that partially serves both dimensions? The mirror does not weigh these for her. What it gives her is precision: financial agency at the cost of connections appreciation, or connections appreciation at the cost of financial agency. Both answers are real. The tradeoff is named. The choosing is hers.

He has spent a decade living inside the gap between who he is and who they believe him to be.

[C1007] Daniel is twenty-nine and gay. He has known this since adolescence. His family does not — or rather, they have chosen not to know, and he has chosen not to force the issue. He grew up in a conservative religious community where his parents are deeply embedded. Their faith is genuine, their love for him is real, and their beliefs about homosexuality are clear and unyielding. He has spent a decade living inside the gap between who he is and who they believe him to be.

In the identity dimension, the questions are stark. Is his authenticity going well? No — he is hiding a fundamental part of himself from the people who are supposed to know him best. Does it truly matter? Yes — the concealment costs him energy, intimacy, and the ability to build a full life that includes both his family and his partner. Is it in his control to change? Yes. He can come out.

In the connections dimension, the answer is equally clear and points the other way. Is his family relationship going well? In its current form, yes — he is close to his parents, loved by his siblings, included in a community that sustains him. Does it truly matter? Deeply. Is it in his control to protect? Only if the current arrangement holds. Coming out risks rupturing the relationship entirely. His parents' beliefs are not flexible, and the community around them will reinforce those beliefs. The path in the connections dimension is appreciation: protect what is working.

Identity says: be who you are. The path there is agency. Connections says: keep the people you love. The path there is appreciation — protect what is working. The mirror shows Daniel both truths with equal clarity. It does something that unstructured reflection often fails to do: it names the exact tradeoff. Daniel does not lack clarity about what is happening. He is facing a genuine conflict between two things that matter, and the cost of choosing either one is real and specific. Seeing it makes the decision his — fully seen, fully owned, and fully his to make.

Conflicting paths across dimensions are more common than the clean cases suggest. A person who needs to leave a draining job for their emotional health but cannot afford the income loss. A person whose physical well-being demands rest while their identity demands achievement. A person whose values call for authenticity in a family that will punish it.

When You See Clearly and Cannot Act

Knowing what to do and being ready to do it are different things, and the distance between them is human.

[C1008] Stuart is fifty-six and has been fighting for his small business for four years. The business — a print shop he built from nothing over two decades — has been declining since the market shifted. Revenue has dropped by half. He has laid off employees he considered family. He has mortgaged his house. He has poured his savings, his energy, and his identity into keeping the business alive.

The questions produce a clear answer. Is the business going well? No — it has been declining for four years despite sustained effort. Does it truly matter? Yes — it is his livelihood, his identity, and his life's work. Is it in his control to change? He has tried everything within his power. The market shift is structural, not cyclical. The path is acceptance.

Stuart knows this. He can articulate it clearly. And he is not ready to accept it.

Stuart can look at the mirror, see that the path is acceptance, and decide he is not ready to walk it yet — not out of delusion but out of a conscious decision that he needs more time to arrive at what he already knows. The picture holds. It waits and remains steady whether you act on it or not. Knowing what to do and being ready to do it are different things, and the distance between them is human. The path is acceptance. The seeing itself is already the beginning of the work, even when the walking has not yet started.

♦ ◊ ♦

When the Answer Was Wrong

She had changed the circumstances without examining the source, and the source had followed her.

[C1009] Jess is thirty-two and spent six months treating the wrong problem. She was unhappy at work — bored, restless, increasingly resentful. She applied the questions: the job was not going well, it mattered, she could change it. The answer was agency. She quit, found a new position, and felt the rush of decisive action.

Three months into the new job, the restlessness returned. Same feeling, different office. She had changed the circumstances without examining the source, and the source had followed her.

When she looked again — honestly this time, without the satisfaction of having already "solved" it — she found that the restlessness was not about the work. It was about meaning.

Both jobs were fine. Neither connected to anything she cared about. She had answered the first question correctly (not going well) and the second correctly (it matters), but she had aimed the third question at the wrong target. "Is my job in my control to change?" was the wrong question. "Is my relationship with purpose in my control to change?" was the right one. A new job was agency applied to the symptom. The source required a different kind of agency — the slower, harder work of examining what she actually wanted to build toward.

Mistakes are still possible. The mirror is only as honest as the person holding it.

Coming back to look again is one kind of difficult. There is another kind, where the problem is the absence of an answer altogether.

When the Answer Is Unsure

Chapter III introduced this problem briefly: unsure is a signal to stay with the question rather than defaulting to whichever answer feels less uncomfortable. What it did not cover is how unsure behaves in the gray areas — where the uncertainty is sustained rather than momentary — a years-long avoidance of the attempt that would produce one. The cases here are that harder version.

The questions produce different kinds of uncertainty, and each requires a different response.

Is it going well? When you are unsure whether something is going well, look more specifically. Ask the question at the level of a facet rather than the whole dimension. "Is my marriage going well?" may resist a clear answer. "Is the ease between us going well?" — "Is the frequency of our real conversations going well?" — these sharpen the picture. If the question is genuinely answerable at a narrower level and the answer there is yes, the overall uncertainty resolves upward. If the more specific questions consistently produce no, the overall answer is no. A marriage in which every facet is functioning is a marriage that is going well. A marriage in which three of five facets are not is a marriage that is not, even if no single facet feels catastrophic.

Does it truly matter? This is the question most often met with genuine uncertainty — and the uncertainty here is almost always informative. What truly matters tends to be recognizable. What does not tends to waver when examined. If you have been carrying a concern for months and still cannot say with confidence whether it matters, that wavering is itself a signal. Apply the test: if this disappeared tomorrow, would your life actually change? If the answer is "probably not" or "I am not sure," the answer to the second question is likely no. Give it a few days without deliberately feeding it attention.

Is it in my control to change? Uncertainty here most often signals that agency has not yet been tested. You assume you cannot change something because it has always been this way, or because past attempts failed. Before settling on acceptance, make honest attempts at change — a direct conversation, an application, a behavior shift. The attempt will tell you more about your actual control than any amount of reflection. If the attempt fails, and the failure is genuine rather than incomplete, the answer becomes clear: the path is acceptance. If the attempt opens something — even partially — then agency remains, and the question is how far it extends.

She has been treating the third question as answered without testing it.

[C1010] Paula is forty-seven and has been considering, for three years, whether to leave her career in corporate finance and pursue the ceramics practice she has been building on weekends — as a livelihood. She has the skill. She has a small following. She has run the numbers, roughly, and they are scary but not impossible.

She holds up the mirror. Is her career going well? She is unsure. It pays extremely well, and the money funds a life she values. The work itself is not something she would choose if money were not involved. She has been unsure about this for three years.

The first question — unsure — points her toward a narrower examination. She breaks the career into facets. Financial security: going well. Intellectual engagement: not going well. Sense of purpose: not going well. The respect of colleagues she respects: going well. The career, held whole, resists a clear answer because it is genuinely mixed — some facets working, some not.

She moves to the second question about the facets that are not going well. Does the absence of purpose and engagement truly matter? Here her answer has been unsure for three years, and the three years are themselves part of the picture. She has not been able to dismiss it. She has not been able to act on it. The concern keeps returning even when she tries not to think about it. When something persists across three years of sustained examination, the answer to whether it truly matters is yes. The inability to dismiss it is the answer.

She moves to the third question. Is it in her control to change? And here she has been telling herself the answer is no — the finances are too dependent on the career income, the timing is not right, her children are still in school, she has not built the ceramics practice far enough. She has been treating the third question as answered without testing it.

The mirror asks her to test it. Could she reduce her hours and grow the practice more deliberately? She has not asked.

Could she set a two-year timeline and begin positioning toward it, so that "not yet" is a stage rather than an answer? She has not tried. The path is agency — not the agency of quitting tomorrow, but the agency of testing the boundary she has been treating as a wall. One honest attempt at change will tell her more about her actual control than three more years of unsure.

When Time Is the Difficulty

The hard cases examined so far are all, at their core, present-tense — a source mislocated, a path complicated by partial control, an answer that has changed. But some of the most persistent difficulties are not about what is happening now. They are about what happened, and what is being carried forward from it. And some are about what has not yet happened — commitments being contemplated whose difficulty lies not in the present but in what they would foreclose.

The question sets for past and future are the same mirror, pointed in different directions, and the hard cases they produce have their own shapes. In the past, the difficulty is usually not in seeing what happened — it is in determining whether anything can still be done about it, or whether the work is to stop fighting what is permanently settled. In the future, the difficulty is usually not in seeing what might happen — it is in knowing how much certainty a particular commitment actually requires before you cross a threshold that is hard to uncross.

The Effort That Was Not Enough

The loss has no deficiency at its source. It has only a margin.

[C1011] Elias is twenty-eight and missed qualifying for the Olympic team by a fraction of a second. He has been training for this since he was eleven. He swam twice a day through high school, turned down an academic scholarship to train full-time, moved across the country at nineteen to work with a coach who believed in him, and spent the better part of a decade building his life around a single objective. He did everything that was asked of him and more. At trials, he swam the fastest race of his life — and finished fifth. Four men touched the wall ahead of him, and the fourth did so by a margin so small it would not be visible to the naked eye.

The difficulty is not that Elias failed. The difficulty is that he did not fail. He did everything within his control, executed at the highest level he had ever reached, and it was not enough. The result was not produced by error, or by insufficient preparation, or by a lack of will. It was produced by the fact that four other people were, on that day, slightly faster. There is nowhere to direct the frustration — no mistake to correct, no effort he withheld, no preparation he skipped. The loss has no deficiency at its source. It has only a margin.

The mirror, pointed at the past: Did it go well? No — not by the only measure Elias has been using for seventeen years. The goal was the team, and he did not make it. Did it truly matter? Yes. This was not a hobby or a passing ambition. It was the organizing principle of his adult life. Is there anything in his control to change? The race is over. The time is recorded. The team has been named. Nothing about the result can be altered. The path, for the result itself, is acceptance.

But acceptance of a past result and acceptance of a future without further attempt are different things, and the mirror insists on the distinction. The race is settled. The question of whether to train for the next cycle is not. Elias is twenty-eight. The next trials are four years away. His body, by every measure his coach and his doctor can offer, is capable of continuing at this level — possibly improving, given that distance swimmers often peak in their late twenties and early thirties. The path for the future is not acceptance. It is agency: a genuine choice, examined clearly, about whether the pursuit deserves another four years of his life.

The hardest part is not the decision. It is the period between the result and the decision — the weeks when the loss is still raw and the temptation is either to quit in despair or to commit in defiance, neither of which is a clear-eyed choice. The mirror asks Elias to wait until the grief has settled enough to see honestly. The acceptance of what happened and the agency over what comes next are both real, and they require different timelines. Rushing the second because the first is unbearable is how people make permanent decisions from temporary pain.

The Commitment That Is Hard to Undo

She should not enter this because it seems right. She should enter it because she has looked at the full picture and is genuinely willing to accept what it costs.

[C1012] Irene is forty-four and has been offered what appears to be the right opportunity: a role leading a small nonprofit doing exactly the work she has cared about for years. The salary is substantially lower than her current position. The organization is small and not yet fully stable. The work would be demanding in ways that are genuinely meaningful to her. She has been thinking about a move like this for a decade.

She holds up the mirror, pointed at the future.

How will this affect the five dimensions? She maps it. Financial well-being will take a real hit — real, and requiring changes to how she lives. Physical well-being is unaffected. Her connections may improve — she has been describing herself as depleted by her current environment, and the new role would put her among people whose work she respects. Her emotional well-being is likely to improve; the flatness she has been carrying is connected to the absence of meaning. Identity: this is where the effects are most concentrated. The role aligns with who she believes herself to be in a way the current role does not.

Does this truly matter? Yes. When she examines the mapped effects, the picture that emerges is one she has been carrying as an aspiration for years. The question is not whether it matters. It clearly does.

How easy is it to reverse if she changes her mind? This is the question she has been avoiding. The financial costs of taking the role are real and will take years to recover if she returns to her field. The career path she would be leaving is not permanently closed, but reentering it at the same level will be more difficult after several years away. The reversibility is moderate to low.

The third question does not tell her not to take the role. What it tells her is this: the certainty she needs before committing to a low-reversibility decision is higher than the certainty she would need for a reversible one. She should not enter this because it seems right. She should enter it because she has looked at the full picture — the financial cost, the instability of the organization, the demands of the work, the tradeoffs across dimensions — and she is genuinely willing to accept what it costs.

If she is, the path is agency. If she finds, on honest examination, that she is not yet certain enough to accept those costs, the path is not to wait indefinitely — it is to identify what would produce that certainty and go get it. A conversation with the organization's leadership about its financial stability. A concrete plan for how to manage the income reduction. A timeline that makes the leap feel chosen rather than panicked.

The Trade That Disappeared

The distinction between adequate and beautiful turned out to matter to almost no one who was paying.

[C1013] Willem was fifty-three and had been a master typesetter in Amsterdam for thirty years when the Linotype machine arrived in his quarter of the city. It was 1893. He had learned the trade from his father, who had learned it from his, and the skill he carried — the spacing of letters by hand, the composing of pages that were beautiful because a human eye had arranged them — was not merely his livelihood. It was the thing he was. He could set a page of Dutch faster and more cleanly than anyone in the guild, and the guild had said so, more than once, with pride.

Within a few years, most of the shops that had employed him were using the new machines. The work that remained for hand compositors was marginal — small runs, specialty jobs, the kinds of commissions that could not sustain a family. Willem watched younger men retrain as Linotype operators, learning to tap a keyboard rather than touch a letter. He could not bring himself to do it. The machine produced technically adequate pages at a speed his hands could never match, and the distinction between adequate and beautiful — the distinction his entire working life had been organized around — turned out to matter to almost no one who was paying.

The questions, applied to the present: Is his livelihood going well? No — the market for his skill has collapsed, and the collapse is structural rather than cyclical. Does it truly matter? Yes — he has a family to feed, and the financial dimension is failing. Is it in his control to change? Here the paths diverge, and the divergence is the point. The disappearance of the market is not in his control. The Linotype is not a temporary fashion. His skill, however magnificent, no longer commands a living. That is acceptance — of a technological change that has rendered his expertise economically obsolete.

But acceptance of the market is not acceptance of everything. Willem knows printing — not just the hand composition, but the logic of type, the structure of pages, the eye for what works and what does not. The question is whether he can carry what he knows into a form the new world will pay for. Supervising Linotype operators who can produce volume but not judgment.

Training apprentices in the design principles that the machines cannot teach themselves. Finding the work inside the obsolescence that still requires a human mind. The path for the livelihood is agency — the agency of building something new from what remains. The identity question is harder and belongs to a different examination: whether Willem can be the man who adapted rather than the man who was replaced. That question has no guarantee attached to it. It has only the choice.

The questions do not change because the century does. A craftsman in 1893 whose trade has been swallowed by a machine faces the same structure as anyone whose expertise is made redundant by a shift they did not cause and cannot reverse. The source is external. The loss is real. The path for the market is acceptance. The remaining agency — the expertise carried into a new form, the livelihood built from what remains — is agency. And the identity question — who am I when the thing I was best at no longer matters? — belongs to the identity dimension, where the path will be agency if he can build a new answer, and acceptance if the answer that arrives is not the one he would have chosen.

What the Gray Areas Teach

What the gray areas teach is not a different mirror but a deeper application of the same one. The three question sets — one for the present, one for the past, one for the future — still work. The four paths still apply. The five dimensions still hold across all three temporal modes. What changes is the effort required — the willingness to apply the questions multiple times, at multiple levels of specificity, across multiple dimensions, and to sit with ambiguity long enough for the picture to clarify.

XI.

The Whole Picture

The dimension chapters applied the mirror one facet at a time. The previous chapter applied it to the harder cases — sources hiding in the wrong dimension, paths pulling against each other, answers that resist clarity. This chapter takes the widest view: four people, each examined across all five dimensions and all three temporal modes — what happened and how to carry it, what is happening and what to do about it, what has not yet arrived and how to enter it.

Four patterns recur in most lives held up to the mirror. The first: mostly good, one thing is off. Four dimensions working, one quietly draining everything. The second: one thing broke and everything followed — a single event destabilizing multiple dimensions at once. The third: everything looks fine from the outside, nothing feels right inside. The fourth: genuine constraints, real tradeoffs. A life that is hard in structural ways where the work is separating what can be changed from what cannot.

Mostly Good, One Thing Is Off

Not performing well — actually doing well.

[C1101] Sandra is fifty-two, divorced for six years, and doing well. Not performing well — actually doing well.

Her body works. She walks most mornings, sleeps decently, manages the minor complaints of a body in its fifties with more grace than resistance. She went through menopause two years ago and came out the other side tired but functional. Her energy is not what it was at forty. It is enough.

Her emotional life is settled. The divorce was painful — the slow erosion kind, where two people who once fit together gradually stopped fitting and spent years pretending otherwise. She did the work afterward. Therapy, honest friendships, the slow process of learning to be alone without being lonely. Her inner life is mostly calm. On a good day, she would call it peaceful.

Her finances are solid. She earns well as a hospital administrator. She owns her apartment. She is not wealthy, but she is secure, and after the financial disruption of the divorce, security feels like an achievement worth naming.

Her connections are real. She has three close friends — the kind you call at midnight, the kind who saw you through the worst of the divorce and are still here. Her relationship with her two grown children is honest and warm. She is dating, casually and without urgency.

Four dimensions examined. Four paths of appreciation. Sandra's life, held up to the mirror, is working. And if she stopped here, the picture would be incomplete — because something is off, and the four solid dimensions have been masking it.

Identity.

Sandra built her adult life around two roles: mother and professional. Both served her well. Both are winding down. Her children are launched — they call, they visit, but they do not need her the way they once did, and the daily purpose that motherhood provided has been replaced by a quiet that she has not yet learned to fill. Her career is stable but has peaked — she is good at her job, she is not growing in it, and she has begun to suspect that she is staying because she does not know what comes next.

The body is part of this too, in a way she has not quite named. She manages the changes of her fifties — the menopause she came through, the energy that runs at a lower register than it did at forty, the face that is recognizably hers but no longer the one in her memory — with the practical competence she applies to everything. But competence is not the same as reckoning. The body at fifty-two is a fact about time, and time is the thing Sandra has not yet decided how to hold. She is not old. She is also no longer young, and the version of herself she reaches for — the one organized around building, acquiring, becoming — belongs to a chapter that is either ending or asking to be redefined. The roles are winding down. The body is changing. The identity is being asked to update on two fronts simultaneously.

When Sandra asks the first question about her identity — is it going well? — the answer is unsure. She does not feel a crisis. She feels a drift. The days are fine. The weeks blur together. She cannot name what is missing, which is part of what makes it hard to address.

The guidance for unsure: look more specifically. She narrows. Values: intact — she knows what she cares about. Authenticity: yes — she is more herself now than she was during the marriage. Purpose: here she stops. She does not have one. Not in the dramatic sense of having lost it — in the quieter sense of never having built one that was hers alone, separate from the roles of mother and professional. The roles were real and fulfilling. They were also structures that someone else defined, and when she looks for the thing she is building toward on her own terms, there is nothing there.

Does it truly matter? She tests it. If this drift disappeared — if she woke up tomorrow with a clear sense of direction — would her life change? Yes. The low-grade restlessness she has been carrying would have somewhere to point. The evenings that feel empty would feel like time rather than absence.

Is it in her control? Yes. Not immediately, not with a single decision, but through the slower agency of exploration — trying things, following curiosity, allowing herself to build toward something without knowing in advance what it will be. The four strong dimensions are not masking the problem. They are the foundation that makes addressing it possible.

Sandra's whole picture, in the present: a life that is working, with one dimension that is asking to be built.

The past: What happened, and how should she carry it?

Sandra was married for twenty-two years. The marriage was not a failure in any simple sense — it produced two children she loves, a version of herself she respects, and a life that held together longer than it should have because both people in it were doing their best. It also cost her years of a slow dissatisfaction she could not bring herself to name until it was too late to do much about it from the inside.

Did the marriage go well? The honest answer is: in parts. Raising children together went well. The financial partnership went well. The intimacy and the fit between them eroded over time until neither remained. She does not need to collapse twenty-two years into a verdict. The mirror asks her to see it whole — to carry what was genuinely good as appreciation, and to stop returning to the question of whether she should have left sooner or stayed differently. The work of therapy and honest friendship has done most of this already. What remains is not more examination. It is permission to stop — to let the marriage be what it was, in full.

The future: What has not yet arrived, and how should she enter it?

The identity question Sandra is sitting with — what to build toward — will eventually produce a direction. Not yet. But it will. And when it does, she will face a different question: how much to commit, and how quickly.

She has been circling a few things she has been dismissing as impractical: a ceramics class she keeps walking past, a mentorship arrangement she was asked about and declined, a relationship she has been keeping at the casual distance of someone who has not yet decided to take anything seriously. None of these is an answer to the purpose question. Each of them is a direction she could walk in, without foreclosing anything else. The future question set applied here: does what she is considering truly matter? The ones that produce a genuine yes are worth entering. How easy is it to reverse if she changes her mind? For most of what is available to Sandra at fifty-two, the answer is: quite easy. She is not considering a second career requiring retraining, or a relocation, or a commitment with major life-reshaping consequences. The reversibility is high, the cost of being wrong is low, and the cost of not trying is the drift she is already feeling. The path is agency — entered without the caution that a low-reversibility decision would require.

One Thing Broke and Everything Followed

Before the mirror, Marco was trying to fix his marriage. The mirror showed him that the marriage was not the problem — it was the fourth domino.

[C1102] Marco is thirty-seven, married, and the father of two boys, ages four and seven. Six months ago, he tore his rotator cuff on the job — he installs and repairs commercial HVAC systems, has done it since he was nineteen, and his body is the instrument his work has always depended on.

The surgery went fine. The recovery has not. He was told six to eight weeks. It has been six months, and the shoulder still cannot bear the loads his work requires. His surgeon says he may regain full function. His physical therapist is less certain. He is in the gap between those two assessments, and the gap is where everything else has started to unravel.

He holds up the mirror to all five dimensions. All five are affected, and he needs to see, in each one, what is actually his to address.

Physical: not going well. The shoulder is the obvious problem, but it has cascaded. He has gained weight from inactivity. He sleeps poorly from pain and anxiety. He has started drinking more in the evenings — noticeably, and his wife has noticed. The shoulder is the origin. The weight, the sleep, the drinking are downstream. Does it matter? Yes. Is the shoulder in his control? The rehab is — he can show up, do the exercises, follow the protocol. The outcome is not — the shoulder will recover to whatever degree it recovers, and that is not something his effort alone determines. Agency for the rehab. Acceptance — for now, not permanently — for the uncertainty about the outcome.

Financial: not going well. His disability payments cover about sixty percent of his income. His wife works part-time as a teaching assistant, and they have increased her hours, but the gap is real. They are drawing down savings that took years to build. The financial pressure is not catastrophic — they are not in debt, not behind on the mortgage — but the trajectory worries him, and the worry has become a constant hum beneath everything else. Does it matter? Yes. Is it in his control? Partially. He cannot accelerate the shoulder's recovery. He can explore whether there are things he can do within his physical limitations to earn income — estimating, supervising, consulting for contractors who know his expertise. He has not explored this because it feels like admitting the shoulder will not come back.

The mirror shows him that exploring options is not the same as giving up. It is agency operating alongside uncertainty.

Connections: strained. The marriage is tense — not about the injury itself but about what the injury has surfaced. Marco's identity as the provider is shaken, and the shame is making him withdraw. He is shorter with his wife. He is less present with his boys. He has stopped seeing his friends from work because he does not want to explain, and the isolation is darkening his mood. Does it matter? Yes — these relationships are the core of his life. Is it in his control? The withdrawal is. He cannot fix the shoulder faster, but he can stop punishing his family for his frustration. He can tell his wife what he is feeling instead of letting the silence fill with her worst assumptions. He can call a friend. These are small acts of agency, and they are available right now.

Emotional: not going well. He is angry, anxious, and ashamed, and the three are feeding each other. But when he traces the emotions to their source, they are not the source — they are the response to the physical limitation, the financial pressure, and the identity crisis. The emotions are real. Addressing them directly — through therapy, through medication, through effort — might help at the margins. But the source is not emotional. It is physical, and everything else followed from there.

Identity: this is where the cascade ends and the deepest question lives. Marco has been the guy who works with his hands, who provides for his family, who can fix anything. The shoulder has threatened all three. Is his sense of self going well? No — the injury has not just limited his body; it has undermined the story he has always told about who he is. Does it truly matter? Yes, and in a way that the other dimensions do not: the financial pressure will ease when he returns to work, the marital tension will ease when the pressure lifts, but the identity question will still be there when everything else has settled. Can he be the provider in a different form? Can he be the capable man who adapts rather than the capable man who endures? Is it in his control? Yes — not immediately, and not without discomfort, but the examination itself is within his reach. He can begin asking what his sense of himself requires that his shoulder actually carry, and what it does not. The path is agency: rebuilding around something broader than what the injury took.

Before the mirror, Marco was trying to fix his marriage. The mirror showed him that the marriage was not the problem — it was the fourth domino.

The past: What happened, and how should he carry it?

Marco has been doing this work since he was nineteen. Eighteen years of showing up, learning a trade, building skill with his hands, and earning a life for his family. He has not thought about those years recently except as contrast — the before, against which the after is measured.

Did those eighteen years go well? Yes. They built everything he has: the marriage, the boys, the house, the reputation among contractors who trust him. They also built the identity that the injury is now threatening, which means the years before the injury are not only something to grieve. They are a foundation. The mirror applied to Marco's working past produces appreciation — an accurate recognition of what those years actually contain, which is more than what the injury took.

The future: What has not yet arrived, and how should he enter it?

Marco is beginning to consider, without yet deciding, whether to pursue consulting or supervisory work — roles that use his eighteen years of expertise without requiring his shoulder to bear loads it currently cannot. He has resisted this because it felt like foreclosing on a full recovery. It does not. Exploring the possibility of a different role is not the same as accepting permanent limitation.

The future question set, applied to a potential career pivot: How would consulting or supervisory work affect the five dimensions? Financially, it could close most of the income gap. Physically, it removes the load-bearing demand while he continues to recover. His connections and emotional well-being are likely to improve as the financial pressure eases. Identity is the complicated dimension: the shift from doing to directing is a real change in how he understands himself, and it deserves honest examination rather than resistance. Does the pivot truly matter? Yes — it is not a small adjustment, and pretending otherwise would be dishonest. How easy is it to reverse? More than he thinks. He would be finding a way to remain in the field while the shoulder recovers. The reversibility is moderate to high. The financial drain continues either way, and the waiting — for a recovery timeline that may shift — is its own kind of paralysis. The path is agency — an exploration begun.

Looks Fine, Feels Empty

He is not happy. He is not unhappy. He is flat.

[C1103] Neil is thirty-one and lives in a city where everyone is doing well and no one is satisfied.

His life, by any external measure, is good. He works in product management at a tech company, earns more than his parents ever did, and lives in an apartment he can afford without roommates. His health is fine — he goes to the gym, sleeps enough, drinks moderately. He has been with his girlfriend for two years, and the relationship is stable and warm. He has friends. He has hobbies. He has everything he was told he should want by the time he was thirty.

He is not happy. He is not unhappy. He is flat.

He holds up the mirror.

Physical: going well. His body works. He has energy. No complaints. Appreciation.

Financial: going well. He earns enough, saves enough, has no debt. He could earn more — several of his friends from college have moved to higher-paying roles — and the comparison crosses his mind more often than he would like to admit. But when he applies the second question — does the gap truly matter? — the answer is no. His income supports his life. The comparison is producing anxiety without producing insight. The path is discontinuation. The energy he spends tracking his friends' salaries and stock options can go somewhere that actually needs it.

Connections: mostly going well. His girlfriend is a genuine good in his life. His friendships are real but have thinned since college — fewer people, less depth, more logistics. There is a loneliness he does not talk about, a sense that the friendships he has are pleasant but not sustaining. Does it matter? Yes — he feels the thinness. Is it in his control? Yes, though it requires the unglamorous work of initiating, showing up, being vulnerable. The path is agency. Not dramatic. Consistent.

Emotional: going well, mostly. The flatness is there, but when he examines it, the flatness is not an emotional condition.

It is a symptom. His moods are stable. His anxiety is manageable. The flatness is coming from somewhere else.

Identity: here. When Neil asks whether his sense of purpose and meaning is going well, the answer is no — and it has been no for longer than he has been willing to admit. His work is fine. It pays well, it is intellectually adequate, and it means nothing to him. He took the job because it was the obvious next step, and the next step after that, and now he is five steps into a career that he chose by not choosing, and the absence of meaning has become the background condition of his life.

He has been compensating for the absence with consumption — new restaurants, new gear, new trips — and the consumption provides brief spikes of satisfaction that fade by Monday. He has been compensating with comparison — measuring his life against his peers' and finding it adequate but not exceptional — and the comparison provides a structure that substitutes for purpose without providing one. Both compensations keep him busy enough to avoid the question underneath: what is he building toward?

Does it matter? He asks himself: if he woke up tomorrow with a sense of direction — something he was building toward that he genuinely cared about — would his life change? The answer is so obviously yes that it surprises him. The flatness, the consumption, the comparison — all of it is filling a space that purpose would occupy if he had one.

Is it in his control? Yes — but not in the way he might hope. There is no test that reveals your purpose, no assessment that tells you what to care about. The search is within his control, but it is a slow and often uncomfortable process. He can try things that interest him without requiring them to be his calling. He can stop waiting for direction to arrive and start walking in directions that feel worth walking, knowing that purpose is often found in motion rather than in reflection.

Neil's whole picture, in the present: a life of genuine appreciation in most dimensions, one comparison habit to discontinue, one facet of connection to invest in, and one identity question that has been hiding behind the comfort.

The past: What happened, and how should he carry it?

Neil has spent roughly a decade making choices by default — taking the logical next step, the expected next role, the path of least resistance through a set of options that were mostly fine. He has been treating this as a source of mild shame: ten years, and nothing to show for it except a functional life he did not quite choose.

The past question set reframes this. Did the decade go well? In the dimensions it touched, largely yes. His career decisions, made by default, produced financial stability and marketable skills. His relationships, maintained with more care than his career, produced a girlfriend he values and friends who are still there. Did those years truly matter? Yes — they built the foundation he is standing on, even if he did not intend to build it. The individual years were not wasted. They were accumulating something, without his knowing it.

The future: What has not yet arrived, and how should he enter it?

Neil is beginning to notice things that interest him in ways his work does not — a volunteer project at a local organization, a side interest that keeps returning despite his attempts to keep it casual. He has been holding these at arm's length because they feel insufficient: too small, too uncertain, too far from a clear answer to the purpose question.

The future question set applied to one of these possibilities: How would it affect the five dimensions? The financial dimension is unlikely to be significantly affected — this is an addition, not a replacement. The identity dimension is where the effects concentrate: even a small investment in something that genuinely interests him would begin to build an answer to the question he has been carrying. Does it truly matter whether he pursues this particular thing? Possibly yes, possibly no — but the question of whether he pursues something is clearly yes. How easy is it to reverse? Highly reversible. He is not being asked to leave his job, change his life, or commit to a direction he has not yet fully examined. He is being asked to try one thing that interests him and see what it produces. The path is agency.

What he has been calling insufficient is actually low-stakes, and low-stakes is a reason to begin, not to hesitate.

Real Constraints, Real Tradeoffs

She does not resent it. She is exhausted by it. Both things are true.

[C1104] Amara is forty-four and tired in a way that sleep does not fix.

She works as a medical billing specialist — steady, adequate pay, a job that asks nothing of her identity and takes most of her energy anyway. She has done it for twelve years. She is good at it the way you are good at something you have done without enthusiasm for a long time.

She is also the primary caregiver for her mother, who was diagnosed with vascular dementia three years ago. Her mother lives with her — there is no money for a facility, and Amara would not put her there if there were. She is her mother's daughter, and in their family, this is what daughters do. She does not resent it. She is exhausted by it. Both things are true.

She has a fifteen-year-old son who is doing well in school and who she sees less than she wants because the hours between work and caregiving leave little room for anything else. She has a partner — they have been together four years, he is patient and kind, and the relationship is slowly being crushed under the weight of everything else she carries.

Amara holds up the mirror, and the picture is not clean.

Physical: not going well. She sleeps five or six hours, interrupted by her mother's needs. She has gained weight. She has stopped exercising — for lack of time. Her doctor has flagged her blood pressure. Does it matter? Yes — she cannot care for anyone if her own health collapses. Is it in her control? Partially. She cannot eliminate the caregiving demands. She can, with effort, protect small pockets: a morning walk before her mother wakes, a bedtime that she enforces even when there is more to do. These are thin margins of agency, and they matter more than they appear to.

Emotional: not going well. She is tired, grieving the slow loss of her mother, and carrying a guilt she cannot fully articulate — guilt about not doing enough for her son, guilt about not being present enough for her partner, guilt about sometimes wishing her mother's decline would end. The guilt is corrosive, and it is also unfounded. She is doing more than most people could sustain. Does it matter? The grief is proportionate and does not need to be fixed — it needs to be carried. The guilt is not grounded in reality — she is not failing anyone. The path for the guilt is discontinuation — release a standard of caregiving perfection that no human being can meet. The energy the guilt consumes is energy she does not have to spare.

Financial: not going well, and the reasons are partly structural. Her salary covers the household, barely. Her mother's care costs money that insurance does not fully cover. She has no savings buffer. A single unexpected expense — a car repair, a medical bill — would require debt. Does it matter? Yes. Is it in her control? Partially. She cannot raise her salary overnight. She can explore whether her mother qualifies for additional support programs, whether respite care is available through community services, whether there are financial resources she has not investigated because she has not had the time or energy to look. The constraint is real. The question is whether she has found every piece of agency within it.

Connections: strained. Her partner is patient, but patience is not inexhaustible, and Amara can feel the relationship thinning. They do not fight. They do not talk, either — not the way they used to, not about anything other than logistics. Her son is self-sufficient in a way that looks like maturity and might also be a teenager learning not to ask for what he can see his mother cannot give. Does it matter? Yes — both relationships are irreplaceable. Is it in her control? She cannot manufacture hours. But she can be deliberate about the hours she has — one evening a week that is her partner's, one Saturday morning that is her son's. Not enough. More than nothing. The tradeoff is honest: time given to one relationship is time taken from another. It does not resolve the tradeoff. It makes it visible so she can choose rather than default.

Identity: complicated. Amara came to this country at twenty-two. She has built a life that her mother's sacrifice made possible, and the caregiving is a form of repayment — gratitude expressed through action. Her sense of self includes being the person who does not quit, who carries what needs carrying, who does not complain. This is a strength. It is also the reason she has not asked for help, has not explored respite care, has not told her partner how close to the edge she is. The identity that sustains her is also the identity that prevents her from getting support.

Does it matter? Yes. Is it in her control? The answer is the one she has been avoiding: yes. She can ask for help without becoming a person who quits. She can accept support without betraying the values that define her. The identity she has built is strong enough to include vulnerability. Asking for help is an act of agency within a situation that has been slowly consuming the person everyone else depends on.

Amara's whole picture, in the present: a life of genuine constraint, where effort alone will not solve everything. Some of her situation is structural — the cost of care, the limits of her income, the hours in a day. Some of it is addressable — the guilt that drains energy without producing results, the health habits that can be protected in small margins, the help she has not yet asked for. The honest line between the two is clear, and her limited energy belongs where it will actually produce a result.

The past: What happened, and how should she carry it?

Before her mother's diagnosis, Amara was building toward something. She had begun taking courses in healthcare administration — not to leave her billing job immediately, but to position herself for a role with more scope and better pay. She had started imagining what her life might look like when her son was launched and her financial situation had stabilized. The diagnosis arrived three years ago and reorganized everything. The courses stopped. The imagining stopped. She has not returned to either.

Did the years before the diagnosis go well? In the dimensions she had time for, yes. She built a career, raised a son who is doing well, and began, for the first time, to plan for herself. Did the interruption of that planning truly matter? Yes — she lost something real when the diagnosis arrived, and she has not grieved it because grieving it felt like resenting her mother's illness. She does not resent it — the caregiving is a form of love — chosen, not imposed. And she can still grieve the interruption. The two are not the same feeling. The past question set applied to those foreclosed plans produces acceptance — of the timing. The timeline she imagined is gone. The destination remains. Accepting the interruption is releasing the energy she spends fighting the fact that the diagnosis arrived when it did.

The future: What has not yet arrived, and how should she enter it?

Amara's mother's dementia will progress. The caregiving will intensify and then, eventually, end. Amara has not allowed herself to think about what comes after — it feels disloyal, as if planning for her own life requires wishing her mother's life away. It does not.

The future question set applied to the life that will arrive when caregiving ends: How will that transition affect the five dimensions? Her time will return. Her financial situation may improve if she is no longer absorbing care costs. Her connections, strained now, have the potential to recover. Her physical health, currently depleted, will have room to rebuild. Identity is the most open question: who is she when she is no longer the caregiver? Asking it now — deliberately — is necessary, and an act of self-preservation. Does it truly matter that she begin thinking toward it? Yes. The woman who enters that transition with some idea of what she wants will be in a different position than the woman who arrives at it having spent the final years of caregiving refusing to look ahead. Nothing is committed to. Nothing forecloses. This is simply the beginning of a thought she has been refusing herself permission to have. The path is agency: small, quiet, and hers.

XII.

Conclusion

You have held up the mirror — to the clean cases and the complex ones, to what happened and what is happening and what has not yet arrived, to what is going well and what is not, to what you can change and what you must carry.

You have looked at your body, your inner life, your money, your connections, and who you are — and in each place, across all three directions in time, you have applied the same question sets. The mirror is now yours.

You have seen its hardest truth: that some things that matter deeply cannot be changed, and that carrying what cannot change with honesty rather than fighting it with exhaustion is not defeat. It is the redirection of energy toward what is still available.

You have also seen the other side of the picture — the one the hardest cases do not show, and the one negativity bias most reliably hides. Most of what you examined was working. The body that carried you. The relationship that held. The financial ground that was, on examination, steadier than the anxiety suggested. The friendship you almost did not notice until the questions asked you to look. All of them require appreciation. Clarity is not only the work of confronting what is wrong. It is also the work of seeing what is actually good — and of letting that register, instead of passing through you on the way to the next problem. The lives in this book that were going well were not going well by luck or by the absence of difficulty. They were going well because someone was paying attention. That attention is available to you. Clarity is seeing the right paths. When you feel stuck, break the facet down to smaller parts.

One more thing the mirror shows, if you look honestly: the life you have been examining was never entirely of your own making. What was going well arrived partly through your choices and partly through conditions you did not choose. What required acceptance was often rooted in circumstances no effort of yours could have prevented. The range of your agency was always shaped by what your circumstances made reachable. This is not an argument against the work — the seeing and the choosing remain yours. It is an honest accounting of what the picture actually contains.

If the book has a simple takeaway, it is this: seeing clearly is not the same as feeling better. But it is the only reliable path.

Appendix:
On the Structure of Self-Examination

If you have finished the book and find yourself asking why three questions and not two or four, why these five dimensions and not six, why the paths are exactly what they are — this is the answer.

I. The Problem

Experience has a structure. It requires a subject — one who experiences — and objects — what is experienced. Without a subject, nothing is registered. Without objects, there is nothing to register. Every moment of lived experience contains both. The subject is singular, while the objects fall into categories — what is felt in the body, what is felt in the mind, what is encountered in material conditions, what is encountered in other people.

A conscious life is a life of change. Change is not incidental to consciousness — it is constitutive of what consciousness is. A being whose experience never changed would have no inner life. Where there is change, there is preference.

Where there is preference, attention becomes consequential. What you attend to shapes what you see, and what you see shapes how you live. But attention is limited. A life seen through finite attention will not be seen whole.

Across every tradition of inquiry into human experience, the same finding recurs: attention is drawn toward what hurts. This is negativity bias — a structural feature of a mind shaped by survival. Without a corrective method, this imbalance leaves good things unappreciated and leads you to spend energy on things that do not warrant it.

To see life clearly, one must account for both the painful and the good. The good is mandatory — part of the structure of experience itself — as real as the bad, and as consequential. A method that begins from problems has already chosen what counts, and that choice is inherited from a bias, not from the logic of examination.

This is the foundation: not merely an observation about how examination must be structured, but a structural claim about what any conscious life contains and what any honest examination of it must account for.

II. The Structure of Suffering

Not all bad is the same. The differences matter, and any method that fails to distinguish between them will misallocate effort.

Certain problems can be eliminated. A job resolves a financial problem. Food resolves hunger. A medication relieves pain. These are problems with solutions, and the solution ends the problem.

Some problems can be managed but not eliminated. A chronic illness can be treated — its effects reduced, its progression slowed — but not cured. A difficult relationship can be improved — its friction reduced, its damage limited — but the other person remains who they are. The bad persists at some level, but its weight can be shifted. These problems produce two paths simultaneously: agency for what management can still address, and acceptance for the residual that no further effort will move.

Some problems admit no solution and no management. The loss of loved ones. The permanent loss of a capacity. An injustice that will never be corrected. These are not problems awaiting the right approach. They are features of a life that must be carried, and the only available response is the manner of the carrying.

Some suffering, then, is unavoidable — the pain of the permanent bad, the residual weight of the manageable bad after every effort has been made. No method can eliminate this. It is the cost of being alive.

But some suffering is avoidable, and it has a specific source: the misidentification of which kind of problem you are facing. Treating the permanent as though it were eliminable generates the exhaustion of a fight that cannot be won. Treating the manageable as permanent produces unnecessary resignation. Treating the eliminable as unmanageable — perhaps the most common failure of all — keeps people in pain that their own effort could end.

A method of self-examination is a clarity method. The ending of avoidable suffering is a consequence of seeing accurately what kind of problem you face — a product of honesty rather than of trying harder or wanting more.

III. The Four Paths

Two sources of avoidable suffering have been established: the failure to see what is good, and the misidentification of what is bad. A valid method must address both. Given these two sources, there are exactly four ways to reduce the suffering that misreading produces. This claim — exactly four — requires demonstration.

The first path is **appreciation**. Negativity bias systematically underrepresents what is working. Correcting that bias — recognizing what is genuinely good, naming it, protecting it — reduces the distortion that makes a functioning life feel like a failing one. It is the correction of a structural error. The good that goes unappreciated is vulnerable: what you do not see, you cannot tend.

The second path is **discontinuation**. Much of what occupies human attention is not genuine suffering — it is inherited anxiety, absorbed expectation, social comparison, the habit of worry that has found an undeserving target. The suffering produced by these concerns is real even when its objects are not. Discontinuation withdraws energy from concerns that do not deserve it and makes that energy available for concerns that do.

The third path is **agency**. When a genuine problem is solvable, solving it ends the suffering it produces. This is the most intuitive of the four paths, and when used correctly — on genuine problems that are within reach — it is the most direct path from suffering to its resolution.

The fourth path is **acceptance**. When a problem is genuine, matters, and is not solvable, the remaining source of suffering is the fight against the unchangeable fact itself. The fact produces suffering that may be permanent. But the fight against it produces a second layer: the exhaustion, the hope and disappointment, the life organized around a solution that does not exist. Acceptance eliminates the second layer without pretending the first does not exist. It is the recognition that energy spent against the immovable is unavailable for what can be moved.

The four paths are distinct and exhaustive. Appreciation operates on what is good. Discontinuation redirects attention from what is not genuinely bad. Agency operates on what is bad, matters, and is changeable. Acceptance operates on what is bad, matters, and is not changeable. Each occupies a different logical position, and together they cover every relationship a person can have with any feature of their experience. There is no fifth option.

The four paths describe your relationship to your experience. They do not describe the origin of it.

What you are appreciating — the functioning body, the nourishing relationship, the work that still means something — arrived partly through choices you made and partly through conditions you did not choose: the family you were born into, the era and place of your birth, the early advantages or deprivations that shaped what was available to you before you were old enough to decide anything. The good that is genuinely yours to appreciate was never produced by you alone.

The same is true of what you are discontinuing, what you are acting on, and what you are accepting. The concerns that do not deserve your energy were often installed by forces outside you — inherited standards, absorbed anxieties, expectations that arrived before you had the language to question them. The problems you are positioned to solve are constrained by what your circumstances make reachable. The facts you must accept often have their roots in conditions no effort of yours could have prevented.

This is not an argument against agency. The work of honest examination is still yours — the seeing, the questioning, the choosing of a path. What changes is the frame in which that work occurs. A life examined honestly includes an honest accounting of what you were given, what was taken, and what you built inside those conditions. Appreciation without that accounting tips toward self-congratulation. Agency without it tips toward self-blame when effort falls short. Acceptance without it can mistake a structural constraint for a personal failure.

Honest examination sees the person and the conditions they are standing in. Both are part of what is there.

IV. The Time Spectrum

A conscious life is not only wide — spread across the territory of experience — it is also long. It runs through time: backward through what has been, forward through what has not yet arrived.

This matters for the method, because the structure of a problem differs depending on when it lives. A present problem is one you are living inside now; the question of what can be done is a question about what is available to you today. A past problem is one that has already settled; it cannot be changed, but it continues to produce effects — through memory, through the emotional residue it leaves, through the patterns it installed — and the question is how to carry it, and whether the carrying is still costing more than the situation warrants. A future problem does not yet exist; it will become real through the decisions made now, and the question is how to enter it — which possibilities are worth pursuing, which commitments are worth making, and how much reversibility to preserve.

The four paths apply across all three temporal modes. What changes is the set of questions that identifies which path is warranted, because what you are examining differs in each: the present is what is currently the case, the past is what has already been determined, and the future is what remains to be decided. One method, three question sets, shaped to three distinct structures of the same underlying problem.

V. The Three Questions for the Present

The present asks: what is the case, and what should I do about it?

The first question is: *is it going well?* This separates appreciation from the remaining three paths. It must come first — before any examination of what is wrong — because a method that begins from problems will find them whether or not they are the right ones. The first question corrects for negativity bias.

The second question is: *does it truly matter?* This separates discontinuation from the paths of agency and acceptance. It must come before the third question, because asking whether something is changeable before asking whether it deserves attention wastes the effort of examination on concerns that should simply be set down.

The third question is: *is it in my control to change?* This separates agency from acceptance. It must come last, after the mattering question has confirmed that the feature of experience deserves the full effort of examination.

From three questions asked in this sequence, exactly four paths follow — a mathematical consequence, not a design choice: the first question has two branches, the second branches the negative, and the third branches that result again — three binary questions producing four and only four terminal paths. Any reordering of the sequence breaks the logic. Any additional question is either an input to answering one of the three, or a consequence of the path already identified.

VI. The Three Questions for the Past

The past asks: what happened, and how should I carry it?

The same three questions apply, asked in the same sequence, producing the same four paths. What changes is the tense, and with it, what each question is reaching for.

The first question is: *did it go well?* Memory is subject to the same negativity bias as present perception. Periods of a life that were mostly good are remembered through their failures; relationships that were mostly nourishing are remembered through their damage. The first question asks the past to be seen whole — before examining what went wrong, examine what went right.

The second question is: *did it truly matter?* Not everything that went wrong in the past deserves continued attention. Old slights, minor failures, embarrassments that felt enormous at the time — much of what the mind replays in the small hours carries no genuine consequence for how you now live. When the answer is no, the path is discontinuation: let it go, and recover the attention it has been consuming.

The third question is: *is it in my control to change?* In the past tense, this question operates differently than it does in the present. It cannot ask whether you can undo what happened — nothing can do that. It asks whether any form of agency still remains: an apology not yet made, a relationship that could still be repaired, a reckoning that has been avoided but is still possible. When agency remains, the path is agency — directed not at changing the past, which is fixed, but at what the past has left open. When no agency remains, the path is acceptance: the past cannot be undone, and the energy spent continuing to fight it is the only part of the suffering that can still be ended.

The distinction between acceptance in the present and acceptance in the past is a matter of what is being released. In the present, acceptance releases the fight against what cannot be changed now. In the past, it releases the fight against what is permanently settled — the energy spent waiting for a different outcome, for an apology that will not arrive, for a version of history that does not exist. Both are redirections of will toward what is still available. The past's version releases what has already closed.

VII. The Three Questions for the Future

The future asks: what has not yet happened, and how should I enter it?

In the present, the questions examine what is currently the case. In the past, they examine what has already settled. The future is different from both: nothing about it is yet going any way at all. The relevant question is how to decide well before committing to what will become the case, and this requires a different sequence.

The first question is: *how will this affect the five dimensions?* Before assessing whether something matters, see what it would actually do to your life. A decision examined in the abstract — a job offer, a move, a commitment — often looks different once its effects across the five dimensions are made concrete. Financial well-being may improve while connections strain. Physical well-being may benefit while identity is complicated. The first question does not require that all dimensions improve. It requires that you see, clearly and in advance, the full shape of the tradeoffs you are making. A decision that enriches one dimension while costing another is not an error — it is a tradeoff. Seeing it before committing allows the choice to be honest.

The second question is: *does this truly matter?* This question comes second because the answer depends on what the first question has revealed. Assessed in the abstract, a possibility may seem significant or trivial; assessed against its actual effects across your life, the picture often shifts. A possibility that seemed urgent may prove, on examination, to carry no real weight. Another may prove more consequential than it first appeared. The first question generates the picture. The second question evaluates it.

The third question is: *how easy is it to reverse this if you change your mind?* Not all commitments are equal in their permanence. Some are highly reversible — you can try something, discover it is wrong for you, and exit with relatively little cost. Others are not: a child, a marriage, a career, a financial commitment that would take years to unwind, a move to a place where you have no other roots. The third question does not counsel against what is hard to reverse. It asks that you know, before you commit, how much of your future optionality you are trading. A high-reversibility commitment can be entered on good evidence and revised if the evidence changes. A low-reversibility commitment requires greater certainty before the threshold, because the cost of being wrong is higher and less recoverable.

The future's questions produce three of the four paths. A future that is not worth entering calls for discontinuation. A future worth entering, with the tradeoffs clearly seen, calls for agency. A future that offers no viable path forward calls for acceptance — and the energy it would have consumed becomes available elsewhere. Appreciation does not arise here, and the reason is structural: appreciation corrects for what negativity bias causes us to miss in what already exists. The future does not yet exist to be missed.

VIII. The Three Question-Sets

To gather what the preceding sections have established:

For the present, the three questions are asked in sequence. Is it going well? If yes, the path is appreciation. If no — does it truly matter? If no, the path is discontinuation. If yes — is it in my control to change? If yes, the path is agency. If no, the path is acceptance.

For the past, the same three questions are asked in the same sequence, in past tense. Did it go well? If yes, the path is appreciation. If no — did it truly matter? If no, the path is discontinuation. If yes — is it in my control to change? If yes, the path is agency, directed at what the past has left open. If no, the path is acceptance of what is permanently settled.

For the future, three questions are asked before committing, in a different sequence. How will this affect the five dimensions? See the full picture — gains, costs, tradeoffs — before evaluating anything else. Then: does this truly matter? The answer is clearer once the actual effects are visible. Then: how easy is it to reverse if you change your mind? Know the cost of being wrong before committing.

Each question set is necessary for its temporal mode and sufficient, given honest answers, to identify the path. The sequences are not arbitrary — each follows the logical priority of what must be known before what else can be determined.

The partial answers — the uncertainties, the not-sure-yets — are not exceptions to the structure. They are signals that a question has not yet been answered honestly. The method's work is to create conditions under which honest answers become possible.

IX. The Five Dimensions

The question sets need somewhere to point. Applied without structure — to whatever happens to occupy attention — they will miss what matters. A map is needed: a structured account of what a human life contains, so that the questions can be applied systematically across all three temporal modes.

The map must satisfy three requirements. It must operate at the right level of generality — common to every human life regardless of circumstance, culture, or era, and specific enough that the questions produce clear answers when applied within it. The dimensions must not overlap at the level of sources: a feature of experience whose source could belong to two dimensions simultaneously cannot be examined with precision. Symptoms may appear across several dimensions, but the source, when traced, belongs to one. And the dimensions must be collectively exhaustive — together covering everything that matters in a human life.

The units of examination are facets — narrow enough features of a life that the questions produce clear answers when applied to them. The map is built not from facets, which are too numerous and variable across lives, but from the groupings that contain them.

The map is derived from the subject-object structure established at the beginning of this essay: four categories of what is experienced — the body, the inner life, material conditions, other people — and one category of who is experiencing: identity. Inductive examination of what human lives actually contain, across enough variation to be confident the coverage holds, confirms that every source of ease or strain traces to one of these five roots. The five dimensions are:

physical well-being, emotional well-being, financial well-being, connections, and identity.

Each dimension holds across all three temporal modes. The body you had, the body you have, and the body you are deciding how to treat are all physical well-being. The relationships that shaped you, the relationships that currently sustain or drain you, and the commitments you are considering are all connections. The self you were, the self you are, and the self you are becoming are all identity. The map does not change with time. What changes is the question set applied within it.

Why five and not some other number reduces to two tests. Can any two of the five be merged without losing something the examination requires? Attempts to merge emotional well-being with identity find that a person can have a settled emotional life while identity is in crisis, or a clear identity while emotional well-being is severely disrupted — different problems requiring different examination that cannot share a root. The same test applied to every other pair finds the same result. Can a sixth dimension be added that is not already contained within one of the five? Proposals for a sixth — spiritual well-being, vocational well-being, civic life — find on examination that each lives within identity, connections, or meaning as a facet of identity. The coverage holds not because a theory guarantees it but because the examination, applied broadly across time and circumstance, keeps arriving at the same five roots and finding them sufficient.

X. The Full Structure

What has been established is this:

Experience has a structure — subject and objects, across time. Attention is biased toward the negative. The bias produces avoidable suffering of two kinds: the failure to see what is good, and the misidentification of what is bad. Four paths address these failures: appreciation, discontinuation, agency, and acceptance. Three question sets, each shaped to a distinct temporal mode, identify which path applies — one set for the present, one for the past, one for the future. Five dimensions map the territory to which these question sets are applied, and they hold across all three temporal modes.

This is the complete structure of honest self-examination: five dimensions, three temporal modes, and the question sets that identify which of four paths is warranted in each. Every conscious life falls within it. Every facet of every dimension can be examined through it, at any point in time.

The method cannot eliminate the suffering that belongs to the permanent bad — the losses, the irreversible limits, the facts that no effort can change. What it can eliminate is the suffering produced by not seeing clearly: the good that goes unappreciated, the undeserving concerns that consume energy, the solvable problems treated as permanent, the permanent facts fought past the point where fighting serves any purpose.

The examined life is what this structure makes possible: a life not without difficulty, but one in which you see clearly enough to appreciate what is good, discontinue what is not worth your energy, act on what can be changed, and accept what cannot. In the present, the past, and the future alike, the same method holds. Point it honestly, and what is there will become visible.

Index of Cases

The cases are listed by dimension. Where a case produces more than one path, both are noted.

I. Physical Well-Being

[C0501] David (53): A landscaper experiencing reliable, functional energy. The path is appreciation.

[C0502] Carmen (44): A professional whose energy collapsed due to compounded habits. The path is agency directed at sleep and routines.

[C0503] Alan (46): A healthy man experiencing disproportionate health anxiety. His body is going well — the path there is appreciation. His anxiety is not going well — the source lives in the emotional dimension, where the path will be agency, or acceptance, or both, once the emotional dimension examination has been completed.

[C0504] Frank (52): A man living with chronic back pain for eleven years. The path is acceptance of the unchangeable baseline, paired with agency in daily management.

[C0505] Lorraine (52): A woman pursuing an external weight standard for thirty years. The path is discontinuation of the inherited standard rather than the body.

[C0506] Dennis (58): A man managing mild coronary artery disease caused by past lifestyle choices. The path is acceptance of the past paired with agency for present habits.

[C0507] Nina (41): A breast cancer survivor still organizing her self-concept around an illness she survived seven years prior. The path is acceptance of the past illness and discontinuation of the cancer survivor identity as the organizing principle of her body-relationship, combined with agency in building a self-concept that matches her present reality.

[C0508] Marcus (46): A man contemplating a marathon. The path is agency, as the future physical commitment is highly reversible.

[C0509] Susan (51): A woman delaying a knee replacement. The path is agency to complete the examination, recognizing the irreversibility of the surgery requires higher certainty.

II. Emotional Well-Being

[C0601] Martin (42): A manager feeling a persistent, low-level flatness. The true source is an unsuited role in the identity dimension, requiring agency.

[C0602] Vera (36): A woman who slowly dismantled the habits keeping her inner life settled. The path is agency to rebuild those specific conditions.

[C0603] Oscar (58): A business owner who rebuilt his life after a partner embezzled funds. The path is appreciation for the present alongside acceptance of the unresolved, permanent anger.

[C0604] Grace (37): A woman with constitutional, managed anxiety. The path is acceptance of her baseline without the expectation of a total cure.

[C0605] Evelyn (43): A woman who reduced her severe anxiety through years of therapy. The path is appreciation to actively maintain the guardrails she built.

[C0606] Margaret (68): A widow grieving a deeply functional forty-one-year marriage. The path is appreciation for the reality the grief points to.

[C0607] Lillian (50): A woman managing chronic depression through a sustained architecture of treatment. The path is active appreciation to protect her management system.

[C0608] Phillip (41): A man trapped by unmanaged depression. The path is agency to initiate treatment.

[C0609] Hannah (46): A woman with treatment-resistant depression. The path is acceptance of building a life that accommodates the condition rather than fighting to eliminate it.

[C0610] James (57): A man processing the death of his father twenty-six years after the fact. The path is acceptance that the delayed grief is arriving at the only opening available.

[C0611] Caroline (48): A woman contemplating cutting contact with a damaging sister. The path is agency, entered with clear eyes about the reversible nature of the boundary.

III. Financial Well-Being

[C0701] Robert (47): A facilities manager living within his means but feeling inadequate compared to peers. The path is appreciation for achieving genuine sufficiency.

[C0702] Raymond (34): A warehouse supervisor unable to cover basic expenses due to structural constraints. The path is agency for what is within reach — examining expenses, pursuing training, seeking assistance programs — and acceptance of the structural constraint that no effort of his can move.

[C0703] Andrea (39): A high-earner aggressively hoarding money due to childhood scarcity. The path is discontinuation of the financial pursuit to address the emotional source.

[C0704] Glenn (50): A consultant who recognizes his wealth is sufficient. The path is appreciation to avoid returning to the pursuit by default.

[C0705] Victor (46): A wealthy man working seventy-hour weeks for money he does not need. The path is discontinuation of the financial goal, combined with agency in the identity dimension to examine who he is without the pursuit that has been organizing his days.

[C0706] Patrick (54): A man who lost his savings in a failed startup. The path is acceptance of the past loss and agency over his current saving rate.

[C0707] Judith (51): An administrator compulsively checking her bank balance due to childhood trauma. The path is discontinuation of an anxiety calibrated for a past that no longer exists.

[C0708] Lydia (43): A corporate attorney evaluating a severe pay cut to become a teacher. The path is agency, recognizing the financial gap is bridgeable and the decision is reversible.

[C0709] Edward (58): A founder hesitant to sell his business despite a transformative offer. The path is agency — the agency of completing the examination the irreversible decision requires before he commits.

IV. Connections

[C0801] Janet (53) & Keith (54): A couple navigating a quiet, highly functional twenty-two-year marriage. The path is appreciation.

[C0802] Renee (37): A woman in a marriage experiencing slow, silent drift. The path is partial agency to initiate repair.

[C0803] Gloria (59): A woman married for thirty-one years to an emotionally unavailable man. The path is acceptance that the specific need will never be met.

[C0804] Sylvia (38): A woman managing an intrusive, critical mother. The path is acceptance of the mother alongside agency in maintaining personal boundaries.

[C0805] Helen (55): A woman sharing an earned, rebuilt closeness with her brother. The path is appreciation.

[C0806] Paul (48): A rigid father whose adult daughter has distanced herself. The path is agency to apologize and change his behavior without demanding a specific outcome.

[C0807] Charlotte (34): A woman experiencing loneliness after moving cities. The path is the slow, unglamorous agency of building new friendships.

[C0808] Walter (61): A man actively maintaining four core friendships. The path is appreciation through deliberate action.

[C0809] Owen (58): A married man experiencing profound, lifelong loneliness. The source lives in the identity and emotional dimensions, not in connections. The path is agency in those dimensions.

[C0810] **Adriana (43)**: A professional facing a deteriorating relationship with her manager. The path is direct agency before considering departure.

[C0811] **Denise (47)**: A palliative care nurse losing her capacity for compassion. The path is agency to rebuild boundaries and enforce rest.

[C0812] **Ian (49)**: A man estranged from his best friend for fourteen years. The path is agency to test a door he incorrectly assumed was permanently closed.

[C0813] **Miriam (63)**: A woman regretting unsaid things to her deceased sister. The path is the hardest form of acceptance: acknowledging a permanently closed door.

[C0814] **Priya (36)**: A woman evaluating whether to have a child. The path is agency, requiring high certainty for an irreversible commitment.

V. Identity

[C0901] **Samuel (54)**: A plumber/coach living in total alignment with his values. The path is appreciation.

[C0902] **Nathan (31)**: A finance professional living out his family's inherited values. The path is discontinuation of the inherited values he has been living by, and agency directed at building a life organized around what he actually cares about.

[C0903] Fiona (60): A woman who systematically shed her performative roles. The path is appreciation for earned authenticity.

[C0904] Keiko (42): A woman living a double life in a traditional family. The path is calculated agency, acknowledging the genuine risk of exposure.

[C0905] Rosa (49): A bakery owner finding deep daily purpose in her craft. The path is appreciation.

[C0906] Diane (47): A nonprofit founder unexpectedly pushed out by her board. The path is slow agency to discover if she wants to rebuild the same thing or pursue a new purpose.

[C0907] Patricia (53): A librarian finding meaning in daily acts of cooking and tending. The path is appreciation — and her case demonstrates why the post-work identity crisis is not inevitable: she built her meaning outside the role, so the role's ending cannot take it.

[C0908] Colin (44): A man experiencing a genuine, pervasive emptiness. The path is agency to undergo deep, likely professional, identity work.

[C0909] Josephine (61): A woman sustained by a tested thirty-four-year relationship with her faith. The path is appreciation.

[C0910] Ruben (33): A successful leader still operating under his childhood label of "the shy kid." The path is discontinuation of the outdated self-concept.

[C0911] Vivian (45): A founder still fueled by a grievance against family who underestimated her. The path is discontinuation of the inherited wound, retaining the drive.

[C0912] Alicia (49): An employee ignoring excellent reviews because she lacks public awards. Her performance is going well — the path there is appreciation, though she cannot yet accept it. The promotion is not going well — the path is agency: finding out what the barrier actually is, before departure becomes the conclusion. The awards require a separate question: if they were only a proxy for the promotion, discontinuation; if the need for public recognition runs deeper, the source lies in identity.

[C0913] Grant (52): A man laid off after nineteen years, experiencing immediate identity destabilization. The path is agency to broaden his identity beyond a single role.

[C0914] Elena (53): A painter who never achieved a public career but maintains a private practice. The path is acceptance of the lost public identity to honor her actual reality.

[C0915] Thomas (46): A man carrying intense guilt for harm caused by his former devout self fifteen years ago. The path is discontinuation of the guilt targeting an obsolete self, alongside agency for remaining repairs.

[C0916] **Rachel (41)**: A marketing executive analyzing a pivot to environmental law. The path is agency, correctly recognizing the narrowing window of reversibility.

VI. The Harder Cases & Whole Picture Integration

[C1001] **Marta (43)**: A woman whose depression is the emotional symptom of a purpose and meaning problem in her teaching career. The path is agency in the identity dimension, directed at the source rather than the symptom. — *"The life behind it has gone quiet."*

[C1002] **Kevin (51)**: A tradesman whose back injury triggered problems across all five dimensions. The path is agency in the physical dimension first — it is the root — with acceptance of the recovery timeline he cannot accelerate, and agency in the identity dimension to rebuild a sense of self that is broader than what the injury took. — *"It feels like everything went wrong at once."*

[C1003] **Catherine (38)**: A woman navigating partial control inside rheumatoid arthritis. The path is a daily mosaic of targeted agency and necessary acceptance. — *"She never knows, on any given morning, which kind of day it will be."*

[C1004] Michael (45): A man who reached acceptance of his marriage five years ago, whose wife now wishes to attempt repair. The circumstances have changed, and with them the path: what was acceptance is now, potentially, agency again. The questions, applied to the current reality, produce a different answer than they did five years ago.

[C1005] Rebecca (40): A woman burned out across all five dimensions, with her career as the source. The path is agency in the physical dimension first — rest, reduced hours, breathing room — before the identity work can begin. The identity dimension is where the other dimensions are being held, and it cannot be examined by a person running on empty. — *"If she is not the high-performing professional, who is she?"*

[C1006] Naomi (44): Conflicting paths: financial agency (take the promotion) conflicts with connections appreciation (protect her children's stability). The mirror shows both answers with equal clarity and names the exact tradeoff. — *"Both answers are honest."*

[C1007] Daniel (29): A gay man whose identity agency (coming out) conflicts directly with his connections appreciation (retaining his religious family). — *"He has spent a decade living inside the gap between who he is and who they believe him to be."*

[C1008] Stuart (56): A business owner who sees the necessity of acceptance but delays the action. — *"Knowing what to do and* *being ready to do it are different things, and the distance between them is human."*

[C1009] Jess (32): A professional who misapplied agency to quit a job when the true void was meaning. — *"She had changed the circumstances without examining the source, and the source had followed her."*

[C1010] Paula (47): A woman who has been unsure about a career pivot for three years, treating the third question as answered without testing it. The path is agency — the agency of making the honest attempt at change that will tell her more about her actual control than three more years of reflection. — *"She has been treating the third question as answered without testing it."*

[C1011] Elias (28): A swimmer who missed the Olympic team by four hundredths of a second after seventeen years of training. The path is acceptance of the past result and agency directed at whether to pursue the next cycle. — *"The loss has no deficiency at its source. It has only a margin."*

[C1012] Irene (44): A nonprofit leader evaluating a future commitment with moderate-to-low reversibility. The path is agency — but the low reversibility means the certainty required before committing is higher than it would be for a reversible choice, and the first act of agency is producing that certainty.

[C1013] Willem (53, 1893): A master typesetter in Amsterdam whose trade is rendered obsolete by the Linotype machine. The path is acceptance of the market shift and agency to carry his expertise into a new form. — *"The distinction between adequate and beautiful turned out to matter to almost no one who was paying."*

[C1101] Sandra (52): A highly functional life with one dimension asking to be built. Four dimensions are working — the path there is appreciation. The identity dimension is asking to be updated: the roles of mother and professional are winding down, and the body has changed. The path is agency through exploration. What is available to Sandra at fifty-two is highly reversible, which means the cost of being wrong is low and the cost of not trying is the drift she is already feeling. — *"Not performing well — actually doing well."*

[C1102] Marco (37): A tradesman whose rotator cuff injury triggered problems across all five dimensions. The physical root is where the path begins: agency for the rehab and the downstream effects within reach, acceptance of the recovery timeline he cannot accelerate, and agency in the identity dimension to rebuild a sense of self that does not depend entirely on what the shoulder can carry. — *"Before the mirror, Marco was trying to fix his marriage. The mirror showed him that the marriage was not the problem — it was the fourth domino."*

[C1103] Neil (31): A successful professional whose sense of meaning is not going well, masked by comparison and consumption. The path is agency to stop choosing by default and begin examining what he actually wants to build toward. — *"He is not happy. He is not unhappy. He is flat."*

[C1104] Amara (44): A caregiver stretched to the breaking point by genuine structural limits. The path is discontinuation of guilt paired with the specific agency of asking for help. — *"She does not resent it. She is exhausted by it. Both things are true."*